ECONOMIC
PLANNING
IN A
DEMOCRATIC
SOCIETY
?

9th Winter Conference

Edited by T. E. H. Reid

Published for Canadian Institute on Public Affairs
by University of Toronto Press

The Canadian Institute on Public Affairs, 244 St. George St., Toronto, Ontario, Canada, is a private non-profit organization, which aims to encourage serious thinking and discussion about issues of major public concern. The Institute, as such, is precluded from expressing an opinion on any aspect of public affairs. Opinions expressed in this publication are not, therefore, those of the Institute.

© University of Toronto Press, 1963
Printed in Canada
Reprinted in 2018
ISBN 978-1-4875-7325-6 (paper)

Preface

The papers in this book are written by the speakers, discussion group leaders, and the chairmen of the 9th annual Winter Conference of the Canadian Institute on Public Affairs. Although the question put to the conference was *Does Canada Need Planning?*, a more general theme runs through all the contributions which can be better expressed by *Economic Planning in a Democratic Society* (the original title of Thorbjörn Carlsson's article). Hence the title of this book. Among the countries referred to are France, Sweden, Germany, The United Kingdom, Italy, the Netherlands, Canada, the United States, and Japan.

The articles suggested a division into three sections. Thus Part 1 contains the articles which centre on *the title* or the compatibility of economic planning with free enterprise; Part 2 those which centre more on the definition or *the nature of economic planning*; and Part 3 the articles whose authors apply the general principles primarily to the question of *what kind of planning for Canada?*

The authors represent an international cross-section of business, labour, and professional economic opinion. For this reason, the reader will find that even though their articles are concerned with similar general ideas and examples, the conclusions drawn vary significantly. Specific terms and examples have different meanings to different observers particularly when the subject involves economic planning in free enterprise systems, which to some implies a contradiction in terms.

Each article is self-contained and can be read by itself. None has a specific title. Instead, it was thought that a statement from each would better indicate the author's approach to the subject. The articles vary in length, some being main addresses to the conference and others short contributions by some of the leaders of the afternoon discussion groups.

The book includes a selected bibliography prepared for those readers who wish to know more about economic planning in various democratic countries.

The 9th annual Winter Conference was presented by the Canadian Institute on Public Affairs in co-operation with the Canadian Broadcasting Corporation at the Education Centre, Toronto, February 8–10,

1963. Like the summer Couchiching Conference (held each year since 1932) it is open to members of the Institute and the public, and brings together over two hundred persons from many walks of life including business, labour, government, universities, and the press.

The Conference opened on Friday evening with an hour-long studio telecast on the C.B.C. television network with presentations by Harry Johnson, Carl Pollock, and Larry Sefton. This provided a background for the discussions on the Saturday and Sunday. On Saturday morning the two hundred participants registered for the first plenary session at which papers were given by James Tobin, R. V. Yohe, Jacques Parizeau, and Arthur Shenfield. After lunch the Conference divided into nine discussion groups to probe into the question raised by the speakers. At the closing Sunday plenary meeting, representatives from Canada's four federal political parties discussed economic planning in Canada in response to questions from the floor. The first hour of this two-hour session was carried nationally on radio and television.

It is with regret that the comments made by the political representatives are not included in this book. The book expanded beyond the anticipated length and consequently had to be shortened. The Sunday afternoon session was most lively and interesting and the Institute is deeply grateful to the four panelists: Mr. Egan Chambers, National President of the Progressive Conservative Association; Mr. Bert Leboe, former Social Credit Party Member of Parliament for Cariboo, British Columbia; Mr. David Lewis, former New Democratic Party Member of Parliament for York South, Ontario; and Mr. Mitchell Sharp, Liberal Party Candidate for Toronto Eglinton, Ontario.

The Institute wishes to thank all the speakers, chairmen, and group leaders who devoted their thoughts, time, and energy to the other participants at the Conference. The Institute is grateful both to the office staff who worked tirelessly for the Conference and to those persons who volunteered a great deal of time before and during the Conference as members of the Conference staff. Above all, the Institute is grateful to its corporate subscribers without whom neither the Conference or this book would be possible.

T.E.H.R.

Toronto
March 1963

Contributors

GEORGE F. BAIN, Economist, Upper Lakes Shipping Limited, Toronto

CLARENCE L. BARBER, Professor of Economics, University of Manitoba

THORBJÖRN CARLSSON, Labour Attaché, Royal Swedish Embassies, Washington and Ottawa

H. SCOTT GORDON, Professor of Economics, Carleton University, Ottawa

HARRY G. JOHNSON, Professor of Economics, University of Chicago

H. IAN MACDONALD, Assistant Professor of Economics,
University of Toronto

ROBERT M. MACINTOSH, Assistant General Manager,
Bank of Nova Scotia

JACQUES PARIZEAU, Professor of Economics, Ecole des Hautes Etudes Commerciales, Montreal

CARL A. POLLOCK, President, Canadian Manufacturers' Association

LARRY SEFTON, Director, District 6, United Steelworkers of America; Member, "Mission to Europe," National Productivity Council of Canada

ARTHUR A. SHENFIELD, Economic Director, Federation of British Industries; Adviser, Planning Programs, British Colonies in the Caribbean

ARTHUR J. R. SMITH, Director of Research, Private Planning Association of Canada

JAMES TOBIN, Sterling Professor of Economics, Yale University; Member, President Kennedy's Council of Economic Advisers

ERIC A. TRIGG, Treasurer, Aluminium Limited

R. V. YOHE, President, B. F. Goodrich Canada Limited; Member, "Mission to Europe," National Productivity Council of Canada

PROFESSOR S. G. TRIANTIS, Department of Political Economy, University of Toronto; REV. M. K. HICKS, Trinity College, University of Toronto; and MR. RUSSELL BELL, Acting Director of Research, Canadian Labour Congress; who were discussion group leaders at the Conference, were unable to prepare articles for this publication.

Contents

Introduction

Planning a conference on "planning" is not a difficult feat. The subject currently lends itself to public discussion, partly because great numbers of people are disenchanted with the performance of the economy in recent years, and partly because there is a feeling that we have missed something that other societies, particularly those in Western Europe, have found.

The Programme Committee of the 9th Winter Conference did not expect to arrive at any acceptable or agreed set of ideas on *how* a democratic society should plan its economic affairs. Rather, we sought to demonstrate that there is a great range of meaning to the word "planning," and, by implication, that we cannot set about doing any planning until we are at least talking about the same thing.

As Alice in Wonderland observed, it is dreadfully confusing to play croquet when there aren't any rules: "The players all played at once without waiting for turns, quarrelling all the while, and fighting for the hedgehogs; and in a very short time the Queen was in a furious passion."

The 9th Winter Conference will have served a useful purpose if it has made people aware how difficult it is to agree on just what we *are* talking about. The contributions in this volume should clarify the issues and perhaps help forestall the confusions which beset Alice.

R. M. MacIntosh
Conference Chairman

PART I

Economic Planning in a Democratic Society?

The State's major choices must reflect the political will of the whole country. Planning is a technique in the service of policy. What matters ultimately is not the technique but the policy. The planning makes it possible to see whether the State is really pursuing the policy that it intends to follow and that it claims to be following. It is not possible to set planning against general economic policy, because the former must be an expression of the latter and an attempt to try to define the true nature of policy. Doubtless it is possible to make good policy without planning if the needs are so evident that there could be no doubt as to what action to take. Where they are not so evident a great deal of information and thought may be needed. In the present circumstances of very considerable uncertainty, of rapidly changing conditions, planning can help to make a rational economic policy possible.

ROBERT MARJOLIN*

*As quoted by A. J. R. SMITH, Session Chairman, February 9, 1963, from the *Action Programme*, European Economic Commission, Brussels, 1962.

Thorbjörn Carlsson

In no country where private enterprise is dominant could central planning be successful without a close and trustful co-operation between government, private enterprise and all interests concerned.

The amount of state intervention in the economic life of the democratic countries of the world has to a very large extent been increased because of a development characterized by a never-ceasing flow of international crisis. Another main course in this respect is the urge for more economic equality among the people of the Western world. Political democracy has thus resulted in an ever-increasing demand for economic democracy, and less privileged groups in society have constantly pressed for more government intervention in a variety of fields in order to bring about more economic equality. Further, our modern societies are characterized by large groups of interrelated and interdependent interests. Frequently, the interrelationship of these groups is affected by competition and clashing interests. Government has often to act as a mediator, arbitrator, and policing force in order to bring about agreement or at least a *modus vivendi* between the opposite and interrelated interests and to get them as much as possible in line with what is considered desirable from the point of view of the nation as a whole. It seems to me that many of the problems that democratic countries are facing today in the economic and social fields and on the labour market stem from the fact that under the prevailing circumstances powerful interest groups are unable to take care of their specific interests in a way that is consistent with the public good. There is no doubt in my mind that if this situation remains unchanged it will be dealt with by more intervention by the public authorities on the basis of legislation.

I think it is accurate to say that state intervention in most instances in the democratic countries has been made reluctantly and often given an *ad hoc* and temporary character.

Such public steps and measures have had to be revised from time to time in accordance with the changing conditions and to avoid the effect of becoming contrary to the original purpose. It has also proved desirable to harmonize and co-ordinate these measures; that is, they

3

have had to be fitted into a planned pattern. As Professor Gunnar Myrdal has pointed out in his book *Beyond the Welfare State*, it has been part of the irony of history during the last decades that planning was often the more "liberal" alternative to the veritable chaos created by unco-ordinated and disorganized state interventions. Thus in situations where withdrawals of certain interventions were not feasible for practical or political reasons, politicians seriously wanting to keep state intervention to a minimum often found themselves advocating central state planning in a number of fields.

It seems to me that no highly developed country can avoid a considerable degree of planning. As a matter of fact, to have a national budget is already planning. Thus instead of discussing whether planning is necessary or not I think it would be much more fruitful to discuss what type of planning we want and how it could best be carried out in a democracy. It seems to me that in no country where private enterprise is dominant could central planning be successful without a close and trustful co-operation between government, private enterprise, and all interests concerned.

But planning is looking ahead, and success is very dependent on forecasting as correctly as possible future changes of markets and of available economic and other resources. Also the reliability of the forecasting will depend very much upon confidence between government, business, and trade unions. I think it is important to underline that only in a society where people have confidence in the future and the feeling of progress is it possible to cope with all the constant changes that are necessary in order to maintain a competitive economy in the world of today.

In my country, Sweden, long-term planning and projections have now become permanent institutions. The first "long-term programme" was set up in 1947 in connection with the Marshall Plan and the greater part of the post-war period has been covered with long-term perspectives.

[Mr. Carlsson uses "perspective" in the sense of "a bird's-eye view." EDITOR]

The latest long-term forecast for the Swedish economy covers primarily the years 1961–5 but covers to some extent an even longer period. This planning and forecasting has up to now been organized on a temporary basis with a new royal commission being appointed for each period. However, the government has now decided to establish a permanent secretariat for long-term planning within the economic division of the Treasury. This indicates that, from the experience gained in the past fifteen years, long-term forecasting and planning have now been accepted as an essential element in our economic development and policy. However, basic methods will remain the same. Plans and forecasting were collected from industrial firms and analysed by the Industrial Institute for Economic and Social Research, organized by the Federation of Industries and the Employers Association—an organization of private industries. Special studies of their respective industries have been made by the Steel Institute and the Pulp Association. Plans and forecasting for electric power have been worked out in co-operation between the National Power Board and the private power corporations. Agricultural development has been analysed by experts from the Agricultural Marketing Board and the Research Institute of the Farmers' Association. Plans for education have been established by various royal commissions and by the Ministry of Education. In such fields as household savings, consumer demand, import propensities, and input/output relationships, the Planning Commission has been able to draw on the work carried out by the National Institute of Economic Research, other economic research units, and individual experts.

The making of the perspective is thus a co-operative effort in which private firms and their associations, public institutions, and specialized research units all take part. The task of the Planning Commission has been to organize this system of investigations and to co-ordinate the material so as to establish an integrated perspective for the whole economy. When the material has been assembled, the Commission reviews it and carries out the final integrated analysis.

The advantages of this decentralized method of operation seem obvious. It has been possible to draw on experts with first-hand knowledge in various specialized fields. Planning and research in certain sectors have been stimulated. Rigidity has been avoided and costs kept down.

Perhaps the following case can be of some interest in indicating the mode of operation used by the Planning Commission.

A survey of the plans and forecasts of a large number of industrial firms indicated that industrial output would increase between 1960 and 1965 by 27 per cent and that industrial employment would increase by 8 per cent. The indication was that this development could be realized without any rise in the level of annual investment. Conferences with groups from different industries centred on the problem of whether these estimates were consistent and realistic. Some doubt developed. In particular, it seemed probable that the need for investment had been underrated. Furthermore, according to a balance established by the Commission for supply and demand on the labour market, industry could not possibly attract an amount of labour corresponding to its expectations. The industrial projections, therefore, had to be revised. Either the supply of factors could be restricted and the growth of production become slower than expected by industry, or investment would have to be increased sufficiently to compensate for a reduction in the supply of labour. This choice was evidently a policy issue. In its final report the Commission recommended the latter and discussed various policy measures to increase the supply of capital for industrial development. The need for capital and labour input was estimated on the basis of econometric studies. According to the Commission's estimates, industrial investment had to be increased by 40 per cent between 1960 and 1965 instead of being kept constant. The result was a shift in the national investment budget towards a growing share for industry.

The most important result of the continuous short- and long-term forecasting is the guidance it gives to the fiscal and monetary policy of the government. In this way, there is a good chance that measures to influence investments will be taken early enough to maintain the economic stability. Also of great interest in this connection is the following: private industry can put a part of their profits into special investment funds of the Bank of Sweden and use this money tax-free when the economic trend makes it desirable to increase those investments which have proved to have a substantial counter-cyclical effect.

A desire to utilize fully available manpower resources, and the necessity to remain competitive in the domestic and world markets, have been important forces in bringing about the long-term planning we now have. Sweden exports about 25 per cent of its G.N.P. and our industries get little or no protection from custom barriers.

Let me finally add that the main thing is that there is created an "image" of the economic future which inspires confidence and facilitates the mutual adjustments of various sectors of the economy. If you ask a private employer about the usefulness of the reports from the Planning Commission, I think he is likely to reply: "The reports give me information about what goes on in other parts of the economy. The forecasts are, and must be, uncertain. But all enterprises have to forecast and plan for the future; and the report provides me with certain landmarks for my own expectations and planning."

Do other free enterprise countries need economic planning? This is a question for each country to answer for itself. In my country, private industry (which employs 91 per cent of the labour force) considers it a necessity.

Harry G. Johnson

Planning of the development council type is consistent with the principles of a free enterprise economy. Planning of the planning commission type is necessarily at variance with free enterprise principles.

By planning, of course, we do not mean planning of things in general by people in general, but a special kind of planning—economic planning—by a specific institution—the government. It is as well to make the adjectives explicit, and to recognize that we are discussing governmental economic planning, in order to avoid confusing the issues. On the one hand, planning is not confined to economics: there can be social and educational and other kinds of planning, and many of the problems to which people seek a solution by governmental intervention involve these kinds of planning and not economic planning. On the other hand, whether the government plans or not, individuals and enterprises in any society are inevitably and necessarily engaged in some sort of planning; the question is therefore not one of planning or no planning, but of whether private planning is adequate to society's purposes, or whether it should be assisted, supplemented, guided, dominated, or even perhaps replaced by governmental planning.

The word "planning" is one of those portmanteau words capable of a wide variety of meanings; the dictionary definition of a plan allows anything from a detailed timetable for a series of specific actions, like a military invasion plan, to a general principle of procedure, such as: it is easier to peel potatoes after you have boiled them. This ambiguity of meaning is the main reason why abstract discussions of economic planning usually become violently emotional—the subject can only be discussed by reference to examples, and everyone is at liberty to choose an example he either loves or hates. It is also the reason why the idea of planning can be extremely unpopular at one time and extremely popular at another: the trick is to change the examples, and it is not really surprising that businessmen who ten years ago were dead against planning—identified with wartime economic controls and communism—should now be in favour of planning—identified with governmental financial aid and moral support for business planning. To discuss planning intelligently, we have to look at examples, either actual working models or hypothetical ones. But before we can do that we have to look into the economic objectives of society and the way planning is or may be related to them; for the purpose of planning is to get things done, and one cannot discuss how to get things done before one knows what needs to be done—whether it is winning a war or serving a dish of potatoes.

What, then, are the economic objectives of democratic societies in which the larger part of economic activity is managed by private enterprise? There is no difficulty in providing at least a superficial answer to this question. Official statements by governments and central banks, and unofficial statements by committees, commissions, and other bodies concerned with public policy, in the United Kingdom, the United States, and Canada, have settled for a short list of four objectives. These are high or "full" employment, reasonable stability of prices, an adequate rate of economic growth, and a satisfactory balance of payments. A fifth objective, too obvious to need explicit mention is implicit in the list: a high current standard of living. And two other objectives are usually mentioned as conditioning the objectives on the short list: an equitable distribution of income and a reasonable degree of economic freedom, the latter sometimes being expressed in terms of adequate incentive to private initiative.

There is no difficulty, therefore, in compiling a simple list of economic objectives for a contemporary free enterprise society; difficulties begin to arise, however, as soon as one begins to probe into the precise content of the items on the list.

In the first place, the objectives as defined in the practices of various countries are not what the words describing them imply. This point can best be illustrated by reference to the objectives of a satisfactory balance of payments and adequate rate of growth. Taken at face value, a satisfactory balance of payments would mean simply a balanced balance of payments; that is, that the country obtains enough foreign exchange by exporting and by commercial borrowing abroad to pay for its imports and its foreign lending. Defined this way, a balanced balance of payments is not an objective of policy, strictly speaking, but a constraint on the country's freedom to pursue other objectives. In the United States and the United Kingdom, however, a satisfactory balance of payments is defined as one that allows an export of capital—loans and donations to other countries—on a scale consistent with what these countries regard as their international obligations. In Canada, by contrast, many people would define a satisfactory balance of payments as one that was balanced without a substantial inflow of private American capital.

Turning to economic growth, one might naively suppose that economic growth means increasing income per head, regardless of how increased income is earned. In most countries, however, economic growth is identified primarily with industrial growth, and with growth of total production rather than of production per head, a definition of growth connected with the political economic objective of increased economic well-being. In Canada, for example, national policy, as represented particularly by the tariff, has consistently sacrificed higher income per head for the sake of increasing the number of heads, and specifically the number of heads bowed over machinery in factories.

In the second place, the objectives I have listed are inherently in conflict with one another, so that a more complete fulfilment of one can only be achieved at the expense of a less complete fulfilment of one or more of the others. Full employment strengthens the bargaining position of labour, and tends to generate wage increases in excess of the rate of increase of productivity, thereby conflicting with price stability; alternatively the pursuit of price stability requires policies that increase unemployment. Economic growth requires using current resources to increase future productive capacity, and therefore conflicts either with the enjoyment of a high current standard of living, or with the objective of balancing the balance of payments without a substantial inflow of foreign capital or a reduction of foreign lending. Stimulation of industrial growth by tariff protection conflicts with the balance-of-payments objective in a more subtle way, since the tariff encourages foreign enterprises to establish branch plants and subsidiaries in a country to take advantage of the protected market. Finally, the objective of economic equality conflicts with the objective of economic freedom and incentive to private initiative, since the pursuit of equality involves transferring income from those who earn it to those who need it, thus dulling the incentive to economic effort for both.

These conflicts between the economic objectives of society mean that economic policy-making is inevitably a matter of choosing how far it is worth while to pursue each objective at the expense of the others—in economic jargon, of choosing the optimal policy-mix. The processes of democratic government, however, are artfully designed to conceal from the electorate both the economic nature of the choices that have to be made, and the economic implications of the choices that are in fact made. Such concealment relies on exploiting the propensity of man in his political life to argue about words rather than things, and to buy policies according to the label attached to the bottle rather than by a scientific analysis of its contents. It is only on this ground that one can understand why various countries have in recent years considered it worth while to increase the normal unemployment rate by one per cent or more in order to check a mild up-trend in prices, or why countries pursuing "national independence" consistently employ protectionist policies that promote foreign ownership of their productive facilities.

It is not our purpose, however, to discuss conflicts between the various objectives of policy and how they are or should be resolved. Rather, our concern is with how the achievement of the objectives is sought, and whether some form of governmental economic planning might be a useful adjunct to the accepted methods of pursuing national economic objectives.

How does a democratic, predominantly free enterprise economy seek to achieve its objectives? Before I answer this question, it is necessary to point out that these objectives, and indeed the very idea that a free enterprise society has objectives distinct from those of its individual members, are a relatively recent historical development, basically a product of this century and especially of the past thirty years. On a very broad interpretation of the development of thought on economic policy, one can say that economic freedom, guaranteed by the laws of property and contract, was the prime objective of the liberal economy developed in the nineteenth century, an objective which it was assumed would carry with it all other desirable things. Gradually, developing social conscience, appalled by the inequalities of *laissez-faire*, came to insist that inequality of property be modified by social legislation and social security, an insistence that culminated in this century in the establishment of the welfare state. Acceptance of the objective of economic equality—or perhaps better, mitigation of inequality—can be dated to the decade before World War I. Price stability as an objective dates from the monetary disturbances during and after World War I. Full employment dates from the Great Depression and Keynes's revolutionary demonstration that a free enterprise economy does not automatically maintain full employment, but that the level of unemployment is a responsibility of government policy. The balance of payments as an explicit object of policy dates from the post-war dollar shortage period; and economic growth has come to be regarded as a policy objective only in the past ten years or less. The adoption of growth as an objective has been in turn the result on the one hand of the cold war and the propaganda value of the Russian rate of growth, on the other of the phenomenal post-war rate of growth of Western Europe. These examples have not only prompted the elevation of growth to a policy objective, but have also—rightly or wrongly—suggested the desirability of some form of planning as a means of accelerating economic growth.

To return to the question: how does a democratic, predominantly free enterprise society seek to achieve its objectives? As I have already mentioned, according to the pure theory of a free enterprise economy, equity, the maximum possible standard of living, full employment, monetary stability, and economic growth can all be achieved simply by establishing the rights of property and freedom of contract, and leaving individuals free to compete with one another within that framework. Democratic public opinion, however, has not been satisfied with that answer, and has sought to pursue the objectives of policy other than economic freedom by more direct means. Broadly speaking, one can distinguish two main means by which economic policy seeks to graft the achievement of these objectives onto the free enterprise system. One is by laws which alter the institutional framework within which individuals and companies compete; the other is by management of the level of economic activity. For convenience, these may be termed framework policies and management policies.

Framework policies include such matters as the use of progressive income taxation and public expenditure on welfare programmes, education, and the like to modify inequality of income and of the opportunity to earn incomes; unemployment insurance, medical insurance, and old age pensions to avert the catastrophes that may befall individuals and families in a society in which economic well-being depends on holding a job; and tariffs and other tax arrangements designed to influence the types of economic activity carried on in the country, and possibly to stimulate economic growth. Management policies mainly involve the use of fiscal and monetary policy—that is, policy with respect to the size of the budget surplus or deficit and the level of interest rates—to stabilize economic activity at some level representing a compromise between high employment and price stability, and to balance the balance of payments.

There are two points worth noting about framework and management policies, as they exist at present. The first is that, at least in broad principle, these policies are non-discriminatory as between particular individuals and enterprises, and are therefore consistent with the basic principles of a free enterprise economy. That is, in principle, income tax applies equally to all people with the same income; unemployment insurance is available according to general rules of eligibility; and monetary restriction affects all borrowers equally by making credit tighter in all financial markets. The second point is that, with certain exceptions written into the tax laws, framework and management policies have not been explicitly concerned with promoting economic growth.

The question is, then, whether a democratic government should explicitly adopt policies aimed at the objective of growth, and specifically whether some form of governmental economic planning for growth is desirable.

According to the pure theory of a free enterprise economy, the answer to both the general and the specific question is clearly no. In principle, the ultimate purpose of a free enterprise economy is to serve the economic interests of its members in their capacity as consumers, and those interests are best served by maximizing the freedom of individuals to choose how to dispose of their resources. The rate of growth, on this principle, should be left to be determined by the interaction in the market-place of savers who want to increase their future incomes, and borrowers who expect to be able to repay their borrowings at a profit by investing for future production. Individuals, this theory asserts, are the best judges of how to divide current income between present consumption and provision for future consumption, and the rate of growth they decide on, no matter whether it is higher or lower than that attained in other countries, is the socially most desirable by the very fact that it is determined by free individual choice.

This simple and categorical view of the problem, however, is not one that can be readily accepted; indeed, the proposition that a private enterprise system will generate a socially optimal rate of growth is the weakest point in the theory of how that system contributes to the maximization of economic welfare. The crux of the matter is that in choosing between current consumption and provision for the future, the consumer and the investor have to base their decisions on expectations about future needs and circumstances; consumers may overvalue current consumption as a result of what economists call "impatience" or "time-preference," and investors may underestimate future profits through excessive caution. Apart from these essentially psychological considerations, there are two other reasons for believing that a free enterprise economy may choose a growth rate below what would be socially optimal. One relates to the presence in the modern free enterprise economy of heavily progressive income and profits taxation; such taxation means that the private reward for achieving growth is less than the social benefit, because the social benefit includes the taxes levied on increases in income, and this tends to reduce growth below the socially optimum level.

The other reason involves some rather intricate economic theory, the essence of which is that economic growth is an unstable process, and essentially a confidence trick that entrepreneurs play on themselves. The theory can be briefly summarized as follows. Suppose that the economy is prepared to save enough to permit a 4 per cent per annum rate of growth in capacity, and that entrepreneurs expect a rate of growth of 4 per cent per annum in effective demand; if the entrepreneurs invest in increasing capacity at the rate of 4 per cent per annum, their investment will just absorb the saving, and the economy will grow happily at 4 per cent, with capacity just matching demand. But if entrepreneurs expect demand to grow at less than 4 per cent per annum, they will not invest enough to absorb savings, demand will fall short of capacity, the pessimistic expectations of entrepreneurs will be justified, and the economy will settle down to a lower rate of growth and a higher level of unemployment than it could have attained. In short, and ignoring many qualifications, if entrepeneurs confidently expect an economy to grow rapidly and act on this belief they will make it grow rapidly; if they don't, it won't.

These considerations suggest that it may be desirable for a government in a private enterprise economy to adopt a policy for promoting growth, not in conflict with the interests of the public, but to serve the community's true interests. But they do not necessarily suggest the need for planning. On the contrary, it can be cogently argued that anything that might be required in the way of a growth policy could be implemented by a combination of framework and management policies. Specifically, by maintaining full employment of the economy, the government could give entrepreneurs the assurance of a growing market necessary to induce them to invest for growth; and by combining a budget surplus with low enough interest rates, the government could raise the rate of growth. In addition—though I am personally rather sceptical of the potentialities for accelerating growth by these means— the government can attempt to stimulate growth by subsidizing forms of investment that have an exceptionally high social pay-off; education, research, and modernization of plant and equipment are often thought to offer such an exceptional pay-off, though the evidence for this assumption seems mostly to be that these investments are unprofitable to private enterprise.

What, then, is the case for planning? and what form of planning, if any, is indicated? In my view the case for planning must be derived fundamentally from two problems of private enterprise investment for growth: the rate of growth to invest for, and the allocation of investment among industries. In other words, the argument must be that some sort

13

of government intervention is needed to establish a rate of growth on which individual businessmen can confidently base their expansion plans, and to work out the implications of that rate of growth for the demand for the products of individual industries and hence for the investment plans of those industries.

The latter part of the job—working out the appropriate allocation investment—is in a sense secondary—a matter of economic arithmetic —although, as the Glassco *Report* and general observation suggest, Canadian businessmen could benefit greatly from more information of this kind. The crucial function is to determine the planned rate of growth; and this function raises the hard questions. Basically, there are two ways of conducting such planning: planning by *bark*, and planning by *bite*.

In planning by *bark*, the government sets up an organization of nationally eminent citizens, say a development council, whose function is to investigate the growth potential of the economy, arrive at an agreed view of what is feasible and what it implies for individual industries, and then publicize its views to the public and the industries concerned, in the hope that everyone will be persuaded to conform to the plan. This is the function of the National Economic Development Council recently established in the United Kingdom. This type of planning amounts to the government lending official support to the confidence trick of growth. The main question about it is whether such a development council can command the confidence that is required for the trick to work. This is doubtful, because the government does not guarantee to pursue policies consistent with the target growth rate; in fact, the development of interest in this kind of planning in the United Kingdom, the United States, and Canada in recent years is precisely the result of governmental failure to provide the necessary conditions for confident business expansion. Nevertheless, planning of this kind might have a significant educational value, in persuading businessmen to take a longer-term view of growth and providing them with information on what growth means for them, and this could both promote growth and facilitate the task of economic stabilization; such planning might also educate the government and the public in the policies required to facilitate growth.

The alternative type of planning involves establishing an expert body within the government, say a planning commission, endowed with enough power—either directly, or through its influence on other departments of government—to force industry to carry out the investment required to implement the rate of growth the planners decide is feasible.

This is planning by *bite*: if you don't conform to the plan, the government will *bite* you. Like planning by *bark*, it involves forecasting the feasible rate of growth and working out in detail, by economic sectors and regions of the country, the amounts of investment that achievement of this rate of growth requires. The difference is that it employs the powers of the state to enforce conformity with the investment programme specified by the plan, especially on the part of the major industries.

If success is defined in the technical sense of conformity of behaviour to plans, the success of this type of planning depends on three factors. The first factor is the prestige of the planning commission, and especially of its chief, with the government and with industry; this is a matter of both technical ability and personality: the success of post-war Dutch economic planning owed a great deal to the immense personal influence of the chief planner, the eminent economist Jan Tinbergen. The second factor is the existence of wide powers of governmental control over industry that can be used to implement the plan: the highly touted success of French planning has been closely associated with the facts that a substantial portion of basic French industry is nationalized and relies on the banking system for finance (which has been provided at heavily subsidized interest rates); and that industry is further subject to various forms of licensing. The third factor, which seems essential to all successful planning, whether Russian or European style—or even Japanese style, which is really forecasting and not true planning—is an over-all inflationary situation on the side of demand, so that the state's powers to restrain or favour investment have a real *bite* to them, and compliance with the investment programme of the plan is in the outcome rewarded with profits.

The background of inflation, price controls, and overvalued currencies against which economic planning developed in Europe is important to remember in assessing the contribution of planning there to economic growth—almost as important as the fact that some European countries have achieved phenomenal growth without economic planning. As my colleague Stanislaus Wellisz has shown, a great deal of the effort of planners in the Netherlands, Italy, and France has been devoted to penetrating the distortions caused by inflation and price controls in order to determine what investments are really socially profitable. This problem, is, in fact, the most difficult in the whole theory of planning. If we look at European planning from this point of view, there is an alternative case for planning in a modern free enterprise economy: planning designed to offset the distortions introduced into the process of growth by the vagaries of governmental tax, tariff, monetary, and exchange rate policy. This, I am sure, is one of the reasons for the popularity of the idea of planning in Canada at the present time.

To conclude, I have discussed the economic objectives of a democratic free enterprise economy, and argued that while the objective of economic growth may call for government action, it does not necessarily call for economic planning of the British or French type. Planning of the development council type is consistent with the principles of a free enterprise economy and might be useful as a way of persuading businessmen to invest for growth and providing them with information on what growth means for their particular businesses. Planning of the planning commission type, on the other hand, is necessarily at variance with free enterprise principles; such planning is a complicated business of using the authority of the planning commission to persuade the government to accept the plan, and the powers of the government to coerce or bribe private industry to comply with the plan. Whether one or the other form of planning, or neither, is desirable for Canada is the question for discussion.

James Tobin

Private implementation of the Plan (in France) involves, or at least threatens to involve, co-operative arrangements among rivals which would be at odds with American tradition.

I can best summarize my paper in advance by posing to myself a series of questions. I shall answer them all briefly and dogmatically, and then discuss my answers at greater length in turn.

1. Does the unsatisfactory economic performance of North America in recent years indicate that we need new techniques of government economic policy, new controls over the economy? My answer is no. Our tools have not been at fault. It is a poor workman who blames his tools.

2. Is the enviable progress of continental Europe the result of techniques and controls unavailable to our governments? Again, I think not. To the extent that European progress in the several countries of Europe is attributable to any common thread of government policy at all, it is the result of more skilful and vigorous uses not of new ideas and techniques, but rather of standard ones, actually ones which were imported by the continent from Britain and America.

3. Should governments plan? I distinguish this question from the question of what powers and controls they need. The answer is clearly yes. Whatever the scope of their powers and responsibilities, governments ought to act with rationality and foresight. This applies to the normal fiscal and monetary tools of our governments, even though their effects on the economy are diffuse and impersonal.

4. Don't we plan now, in this sense of the word, and if not, why not? In the United States at least, we have not geared fiscal and monetary policy sufficiently to our principal economic objectives, simply because we have constrained them unnecessarily by subordinate and irrelevant rules, such as trying to balance the budget.

5. Does government planning require long-run economic projections, to which the government is in some degree committed? I believe the answer is yes. Our governments are inevitably engaged in a number of activities which require long-run economic projections. And a central

17

government can scarcely make a serious projection to which it does not in some degree commit its influence on economic events.

6. Should a projection of this kind be made known to the private economy and, indeed, made with the co-operation of private economic groups? I think that this would be desirable. I believe—and French experience seems to confirm—that a consensus on the broad outlines of the economic future has some tendency to fulfil itself. This self-fulfilling power eases the task of government fiscal and monetary policy. At the same time, we are clearly some years away from the degree of mutual trust between government and business, and between conflicting private economic groups, which will be necessary to develop a consensus projection. Meanwhile, the task of improving our economic performance falls on the more traditional tools of government policy. And I repeat that I believe them adequate to do almost all the job.

Now I shall discuss these points in turn.

First, economic performance in North America has certainly been unsatisfactory in recent years. Persistent unemployment, excess capacity, sluggish growth, and balance of payments difficulties are clear symptoms. But this failure is not in any significant degree a technical failure of the instruments of economic policy. Disappointing as our economic performance has been, it does not indicate urgent need for new techniques of government control over the economy or new politico-economic institutions. The failure has rather been a failure of policy and of politics. We have simply not used properly and vigorously the tools of economic policy which our democracies already have. Nothing in the record of the last decade indicates that it was beyond the present and traditional economic powers of our governments to achieve full employment and a faster rate of economic progress. The fault has not been in the machinery, but in its operation. In particular, I have little doubt that more timely, flexible, and vigorous use of budgetary and tax measures, and of monetary and debt management powers, could have achieved substantially higher rates of employment and utilization of capacity in the last five or six years. These broad governmental controls over aggregate demand could certainly have shortened recessions and lengthened recoveries; they might well have avoided altogether our most recent recession. Higher utilization and employment would have, in my opinion, contributed substantially to solving our other difficulties: slow growth and balance of payments deficits. For they would have increased both the incentives for private investment—in North America rather than in Europe—and the profits available to finance such investment.

At the same time, the provision of adequate, and adequately growing, demand would have solved or at least muted the host of so-called structural problems which cry so dramatically for special *ad hoc* solutions today. I refer to depressed areas, so-called technological unemployment resulting from automation, the alleged profit squeeze, and the well-publicized competitive difficulties of numerous American industries, especially those manufacturing hard goods. I hazard the guess, or perhaps the assertion, that these structural problems would appear much less formidable and intractable if business and labour could adapt to them in an environment of full employment—with aggregate demand sufficient to maintain full utilization. They would appear then in their real light, as the normal growing pains of a progressive free economy. What is troublesome is to have the pains and not the growth.

With reference to the second point, the more successful economic performance of Western European countries has, of course, numerous causes, many of which have nothing to do with government policy. For example, they had a favourable exchange rate set in 1949. But government policy has helped, and we are entitled to ask how. Europe has been growing faster and accumulating reserves. Europe seems to have conquered the trade cycle, or at least to have converted its downswing into a phase of continued but somewhat slower expansion. These successes have occurred in European countries which differ widely in degree and kind of government intervention in the private economy—in Germany as well as France, in Scandinavia as well as Italy.

I have been a little concerned to hear references made to continental European planning, as if all continental European countries are engaged in the same kind of economic policies and institutions. The Germans have nothing like the French operations for planning and they do not want to have, at least they have not wanted to have, and their progress has been good too. So I do not think you can make a generalization that there is a kind of single continental European system of planning which has been responsible for their success. Various continental countries have had great success and with varying degrees and kinds of government intervention in the economy. If these countries have anything in common in the realm of public economic policy, it is not that they are novel techniques of planning so far unavailable in North America. It is that they use fiscal and monetary policies flexibly and unashamedly as means of balancing aggregate demand and supply. They have taken seriously and applied regularly what was originally an Anglo-American economic idea: national budgeting of productive resources against the demands upon them, or, if you like, the balancing of national saving at full employment against national investments and other private and public uses of saving. In those governments, the economic and budget message every year naturally explains how the total demand during the year will be balanced by the resources that the economy has available to satisfy them. This idea has not gained public acceptance on this side of the Atlantic. The Europeans have demonstrated that it works, and their experience supports my first point: namely, that most of what is wrong with the North American economy could be remedied if our present instruments of budget, tax, monetary, and debt management policies were fully dedicated to this purpose.

Third, naturally governments have to plan. After all, planning means no more than acting rationally, basing current decisions on informed estimates of their future consequences and appraising the consequences of alternative decisions in terms of a consistent set of objectives. A government has to plan, whether its powers and controls over the economy are limited or extensive, indirect or direct, diffuse or specific. Any modern government has, at a minimum, a budget involving expenditures and taxes, and in addition the monetary powers of a sovereign state. These instruments have to be used and the only question is whether their use is planned with an eye to economic effects or not. Some governments also exercise a wide range of specific controls, that is, detailed interventions into private economic decisions. These too can be exercised blindly and often are. Or they can be the means of implementing and enforcing a detailed government plan as perhaps they have been in France. Even in the United States and Canada there are a large number of specific controls, but they usually have very specific purposes, or cross-purposes. They concern public health and safety, or competitive positions, or utility rates, or farm production and subsidy, and so on. They are not available for directing the general course of the economy.

It is a great mistake to confuse planning and controls. I have said above that I regard the fairly limited arsenal of general controls at the disposal of the governments of our countries as adequate to the task of improving our over-all economic performance. These controls are, by and large, by-products of the fiscal and monetary operations of the government. Their effects on the economy are diffuse and indirect. They do not involve specific and coercive interventions in the economic decisions of business firms and households. They are, nonetheless, very powerful regulators of the over-all level of demand. But these controls will be adequate only if their use is planned to achieve the economic objectives we seek.

Fourth, the major obstacles to the intelligent use of the tools of general economic policy we already have is that we divert these tools to the service of false goals. The problem of economic policy is complicated enough when we confine ourselves to true goals. For the true goals sometimes conflict, and it certainly requires skilful management and planning to use the available tools in just the right combination to achieve several objectives at once. It becomes nearly impossible when extraneous goals are introduced, when ends become confused with means, when subordinate goals acquire vested status. If fiscal policy must serve an objective of accounting balance, elevated to the status of the touchstone of financial responsibility by a combination of misunderstanding and political ideology, the fiscal policy is not free to promote full employment and economic expansion. If central banks are more concerned with the technical characteristics of bond markets than with the health of markets for goods and services, they are not wholly free to stabilize the economy or even to manage the balance of payments. If governments place more emphasis on the external symbols of prestige than on the substance of prosperity, or if they insist on tying their own hands by non-functional rules—like our debt limit or our domestic gold cover requirement—they severely limit the possibility of using economic policy instruments for economic goals.

Lest I be misunderstood, I would add that it is not a question of substituting economists' goals for the goals of the nation. There is ample evidence that the American people do want full employment, full production, and faster economic growth. These objectives are enshrined in a historic declaration of U.S. national policy, the Employment Act of 1946. If lesser objectives are nevertheless placed in their road, it is because of a wide misunderstanding of economic mechanisms rather than a shift in basic values.

Fifth, there are many specific responsibilities of government which obviously require economic projections, often fairly long-term projections. Surely private businesses with similar responsibilities would find such projections indispensable. Our governments are, for example, in the business of education. They must plan for the school and university enrolments of the future, and provide both for the physical facilities and the teachers that will be needed. They must gear the kind of education and vocational training they offer to future occupational demands. It makes little sense, for example, to devote immense resources to training more farmers in North America, or to launch new programmes of medical care without also providing for an adequate supply of physicians. Similarly, our governments provide highways, airports, and other modes of transportation; they provide parks, camp grounds, and other recreational facilities; they develop water resources for power and irrigation, and for industrial and home use; they have a major responsibility for hospitals and medical research. To plan all these activities and many more they need economic projections—no less than a private telephone company planning its long-range investments. An economic projection is, of course, not *per se* a plan; it does not become so unless the government is also committing its instruments of policy to the realization of the projection.

Finally, it is clear that the many long-range programmes of governments are interrelated, and there are obvious advantages in basing them on a common view of the economic future, at least in its broad outlines. It is scarcely efficient for example, to have one arm of the government reclaiming land for agricultural use while another is buying land elsewhere out of production. And if the various branches of governments are to plan consistently and intelligently from a common projection, it is certainly foolish for them to use a projection which the government itself has no intention of trying to realize. A government projection can scarcely be a detached, academic guess about the economic future. A common view of the economic future, to which the government feels some degree of commitment, can improve not only intra-government planning but also private planning. That is, it can improve the over-all results of the diffuse and decentralized set of plans and decisions which run a free economy. For, as a general rule, information can do no harm, and may do good. It may do good in two ways. The first is to avoid mistakes in the allocation of resources—in the direction of investment and enterprise, or in individual choices regarding education and careers. The second is that, to a certain extent, a widely disseminated economic projection representing not only the guess of the government, but its programme, will be self-fulfilling. For if businessmen individually have confidence that the markets will be there, they will make the investments which collectively help to provide those very markets.

I certainly do not mean that mutual confidence can make *any* plan self-fulfilling. A projection must be feasible and self-consistent in its assumptions about technological possibilities and economic behaviour. But if it meets these requirements, its chances of realization are certainly improved if it accords with business and consumer expectations. In all the respects mentioned, the French Plan appears to be quite successful. Confidence in the plan stems from the fact that it does make coherent economic sense, and partly from the government's commitment to it, and partly from the participation of the business community and other sectors of the private economy in the making of the projections. This participation means that the planning organization is something of a mutual confidence society: I expand by 5 per cent or 6 per cent because I think you will too. The importance of this kind of mutual confidence—confidence among businessmen, and between businessmen and government—is especially great when a general raising of sights is called for. This was the case in France right after the war, and it was Jean Monnet's great achievement to induce French industrialists to start thinking big, overcoming cautions bred by decades of stagnation, depression, and war.

While we can learn a great deal from the French experiment, I believe the main lessons applicable to North American institutions concern the informational aspects (the indicative aspects) of the French Plan, rather than the techniques of implementation.

Many of these techniques involve detailed governmental controls and subsidies which our governments neither have nor want. A much larger part of economic activity is under direct state management in France. And with respect to private industry, the French government is, in a sense, engaged in a continuous process of negotiations for which the Plan provides useful standards and guideposts. Finally, private implementation of the Plan involves, or at least threatens to involve, co-operative arrangements among rivals which would be at odds with American tradition, the sort of tradition we have in anti-trust laws. I do not believe that the benefits of the Plan in raising sights and in making expectations more consistent are wholly dependent on these techniques of implementing it.

After six years of slack, slow growth, and periodic recession in North America, our businessmen are naturally sceptical of the future—increasingly so, the longer the sluggishness continues. A revolution in expectations is needed if they are to provide the investments required for faster growth and for full utilization of steadily growing capacity. Government policies can accomplish such a revolution in time, as they actually improve the economy. But when business investors are sceptical about expansion, as they obviously were in the United States in 1962, fiscal and monetary policies have to be all the more vigorous to bring about the expansion. And this means they have to be all the more offensive to some of the irrational and ideological viewpoints I mentioned earlier. For this reason, it would be very useful, if it were possible, to accompany expansionary government policies, like President Kennedy's tax proposals, with a common economic projection representing at the same time the government's over-all programme and the co-operative forecasting efforts of government and the private economy.

How detailed need such a projection or plan be? Clearly a mere statement about the rate of growth of G.N.P. is not sufficient. President Kennedy has made 4½ per cent growth a government target in the United States, and we have joined with Canada and the other nations of the O.E.C.D. in setting a collective goal of increasing output by 50 per cent over the present decade. These commitments are desirable in setting a general climate. But they need to be translated into sub-aggregates closer to the planning needs and processes of business firms and individuals—and of government agencies themselves, for that matter. But, at the other extreme, I do not think we need the immense detail or spurious appearance of precision involved in a mammoth input-output table.

Unfortunately, unlike France, we in the United States probably do not have the degree of mutual trust necessary for such an undertaking. Government, by whatever political party, is intrinsically suspect. Large and influential segments of American opinion do not believe government should have any economic policy at all. In this atmosphere, it is unlikely that the Monnet kind of miracle could be wrought in time to be of much help. Perhaps the only way we can learn again what a dynamic full employment economy is like is to experience it for a while. This does not mean we should not work meanwhile to develop a larger consensus of the desirable and feasible economic future. There would be two very valuable by-products of such an effort, which would make it pay off even before it was completed. One would be to give the business community and the public at large a greater understanding of the macroeconomic problems that face the government. Another would be to dramatize the community of interest in high rates of utilization and expansion, which create higher incomes of all kinds, profits as well as wages. But at least for a few years, expectations cannot be sufficiently altered to reduce the need for decisive and vigorous fiscal and monetary policies. These will have to do the job, and fortunately it is not beyond their reach.

PART II

The Nature of Economic Planning

Economic planning is not a panacea for solving problems. Rather it is a means for avoiding ignorance and incoherence in policy formulation. Essentially its purpose is not to determine the choices to be made between courses of policy action but first to clarify economic objectives, second to project the outcome of past, present, and future decisions and third to serve as a basis for helping to assure that these decisions remain consistent with each other and with the economic objectives which are to be accepted for a nation.

ROBERT MARJOLIN*

*As paraphrased by A. J. R. Smith, Session Chairman, February 9, 1963, from the *Action Programme*, European Economic Commission, Brussels, 1962.

Robert M. MacIntosh

Planning is not good industrial relations. The search for better industrial relations is not any the less important an economic technique. But it is a different technique.

Has planning been a significant factor in the relatively high rates of growth experienced in Western Europe and in Japan in the last decade? If so, is European practice relevant to the North American economy?

Planning has probably been a factor in the swift rise of the Western European economy in recent years, but it is given a great deal more credit than it deserves. The following are some of the more obvious contributing factors:

(*a*) the Marshall plan contributed enormously to the reconstruction and modernization of European industrial capacity;

(*b*) the return of de Gaulle to power in France helped provide an atmosphere of political stability in which businessmen could plan;

(*c*) the economy of West Germany benefited greatly from a steady influx of labour from East Germany on the one hand, and freedom from heavy defence burdens on the other;

(*d*) perhaps most important, Western Europe faced up to the challenge of survival as a "third force" in a world of two great powers, and somehow developed a will to overcome great obstacles. This new spirit of determination led to the Coal and Steel Authority and to the Common Market, each success reinforcing the will to succeed again. A new emphasis on efficiency replaced, to some degree, the entanglement of protection surrounding all sorts of vested interests. The concept of planning is to some extent the outgrowth of this new spirit, which found its early application in the rationalization of the coal and steel community.

There is a certain amount of fadism in the search for "planning." The public is very apt to be moved by the latest popular economic cliché. It is only a matter of five or six years since "growth" was all the rage, and the Canadian public was treated to a stunning revelation of the broad economic vistas opening towards 1980. What happened to growth? Unfortunately the professional economists as well as the lay public are apt to be carried away with admiration for their own *assumptions* and to start calling them *conclusions*.

The first thing to be said about economic planning is that we cannot assume its usefulness until we know just what it is we are talking about. The great range of views on the scope and nature of economic planning displayed at the Conference shows clearly enough that, to avoid confusion, we have to begin at the beginning, which is at the point where we attempt to reach agreement on what it is we are talking about.

It has to be said that confusion as to what planning means is not likely to be dispelled by the *Report* of the Mission to Europe which was carried out under the auspices of the National Productivity Council. One gets the impression from this *Report* that planning is primarily concerned with responsible and warm-hearted relations between labour and management. Undoubtedly this is a social objective which is very much to be desired, and it may well be one about which we have much to learn from the Swedes and the Dutch. But I am not at all sure that it has very much to do *directly* with planning, although it should be obvious that confident, friendly, and trustworthy techniques of negotiation between labour and management are good in themselves, regardless of what sort of economic policy is being followed.

Bargaining over the division of the national pie is not, however, something which can be left for business and labour to work out by themselves. There are a good many other competing economic interests in society, such as agriculture and the two-thirds of the labour force which is non-unionized. "Planning," in the sense of setting economic goals which labour and management agree to and try to implement by responsible behaviour, is necessarily something which involves the government. And government is, by definition, the great forum which represents *all* the competing economic and political interests in society. It is therefore government, not labour and management as independent entities, which decides on economic goals and introduces (we hope) policies designed to attain the politically agreed objectives. The distinction is an important one, because the peculiar idea has got loose that if only government would stay out of planning, then we could get on with the job. There is the related idea that government, labour, business, and agriculture represent a sort of four-sided group who sit down and haggle things out. In this little bridge club, exactly who is the government supposed to represent—all groups other than labour, business, and agriculture? Even to set this idea down on paper is to show how woolly it is; government represents *all* these interests, which incidentally may and often do overlap among themselves. So government is scarcely one of four equal partners; it represents the ultimate authority, all the people.

So the first thing to be clear on is that planning is *not* good industrial relations. In order to avoid misunderstanding on this point, I want to emphasize that the search for better industrial relations is not any the less important an economic technique; in fact it may well be more important. But it is a *different* technique. Confusion on this point has led some people to think that planning is just a matter of getting men of goodwill to sit down around a bargaining table, as representatives of various interests, and agree to be reasonable. Canada and other countries including France have one or more bodies of this character, and the simple truth is that these bodies do not have, and were never meant to have, executive (or analytical) power of any kind. They are talking shops, in the pleasant sense of the word; that is, they are meant to be vehicles where various organized bodies of economic opinion can make their general views felt.

When it comes to policy, this has to be decided by the government of the day, resting on its constitutional authority. And if the government is going to make good policy, it will require among other things a staff of professional economic advisers. One question at issue is: could the government make better policy if it had a special division (a Planning Board or Development Board or whatever) responsible for trying to gather up and understand the sum total of the plans and decisions of private and public corporations and people throughout the country? The *machinery* of such a board would certainly involve extensive consultation with businessmen on their investment plans, just to ascertain what they are doing. The board would look for inconsistencies or incompatabilities in the plans of private citizens. It might recommend to government that such differences be ironed out, and of course, it would be up to government to iron them out by the use of such incentives or restraints as it thought appropriate.

Where business, labour, and agriculture might fit into this set-up is in providing such a board with their voluntary services in collecting and co-ordinating information. The whole point of developing this type of planning machinery would be to gain the positive and whole-hearted co-operation of these organized interests, both for the value of the information they can produce, and for making them participants in the process of arriving at economic policy. There might be some reason to hope that in the process of collecting and co-ordinating information, obvious inconsistencies or bottlenecks would be voluntarily corrected by the decisions of private individuals and firms. If not, they would have to be settled where they are always settled anyway, at the top—at government level.

The trouble is that in Canada we have two tops, two levels of government. A great many of the problems in economic co-ordination which this country faces in the future will revolve around the division of government responsibility between federal and provincial levels, rather than between government and private sectors of the economy. This point receives some acute attention in one of the papers in the last section. If the reader is not sure when he has finished this volume exactly what the answers are to this and other problems, at least we can hope that he will be able to pose the right questions.

Arthur A. Shenfield

. . . we define the essence of planning as the contrived co-ordination of economic activity by means of a centralized initiative.

It is a pity that all discussions on planning, economic or otherwise, must begin with a demand for definitions, but it cannot be helped. To the question "Does Canada Need Planning?" I have to reply, without any desire for obfuscation, "If you will first tell me what planning is, I will tell you whether Canada—or Timbuctoo, for that matter—needs it." Of course there are those who will be irritated by this. For them "planning" is a magic word, the efficacy of which for the improvement of our economic affairs should be apparent to the meanest intelligence —and would be, if only economists did not ask over-sophisticated questions. Unfortunately this will not do; for whether planning is as planning does, or whether planning is what planners say it is, there are numerous alternatives to choose from. And to know what we are talking about is a not unreasonable condition of discourse.

Unfortunately planning is one of the slipperiest of concepts. If one thinks at any time that one has pinned a planner down to some manageable definition, one finds that he has meanwhile slid away to another definition. Or alternatively he presents a definition which can mean anything or everything. Yet again, there are those who, because they believe in planning, also believe that everything they do is planning. An excellent example of this type of planner is to be found in the British Labour Government of 1945–51. Apart from the continuation of wartime economic controls, there was nothing in what they did which bore the mark of planning. In the main it was no more than a succession of lurches from one expedient to another. Yet Labour believed that it was a great planner simply because it believed in planning.

Is planning the mere exercise of forethought? If so, we must all be for it and we need take our discussion no further. Is it the pursuit of some national economic goal? This perhaps gets a little nearer to the real thing, at least in a pejorative sense, for the pursuit of a national economic goal itself has a faintly totalitarian flavour. However, I have to admit that even a nation with the most free economy has a national goal, if it is only the maximization of individual economic freedom; and so I must accept the pursuit of a national economic goal as possibly desirable, but it hardly lends itself to further analysis. Is planning simply the performance of the normal tasks of government with above-normal intelligence, follow-through, or intelligibility? This, too, we must of course readily accept and in doing so we once again close down the discussion.

It seems to me that discussion can become fruitful only if we define the essence of planning as *the contrived co-ordination of economic activity by means of a centralized initiative.* The planning state takes action to co-ordinate the economy, and in so doing to guide or direct it, over and above the action required to produce a legal framework for the market. Of course there are ambiguities in this. Most laws relating to property, trade, and industry are clearly part of a legal framework for a free market. But are anti-trust laws a protection for the free market or a planned interference with it? Still more, is the control of the money supply, interest rates, and banking practices the impartial work of a referee or is it the power-loaded play of the coach? There are no precise answers to this.

However, if I may use a hackneyed but still helpful expository device, though I cannot give a precise definition of an elephant, I know one when I see one. And when I see the state saying, over a substantial part of the economy, "You must (or at least we should like you to, and if you are good we are sure you will) produce what we choose, not what you or your customers choose; and leave the dovetailing of all this into an harmonious whole to us, not to the market," then I know I am looking at a case of economic planning.

Why should it be thought that Canada or any other free enterprise economy may need this? Because they have problems—unemployment, slow growth, balance of payments difficulties, and others. But why should it be thought that economic planning can solve these problems? Here are some of the popular answers. First, the French have done it; the Dutch, Italians and Japanese are doing it; and the British are about to do it. And look at the French, Dutch, Italian, and Japanese rates of growth, or even the less but quite respectable rate of growth which the British planners believe they can produce!

Secondly, the market cannot do the job we need. Dovetailing into an harmonious whole is what the textbook market does but what the real market conspicuously fails to do. Growth comes through the market only sporadically and shakily. What we need is sustained and sure-footed growth.

Thirdly, in Canada's particular case, the economy is a very special creature, needing very special treatment such as only a centralized initiative can deliver. Here are ten provinces strung out over an immensely long but perilously thin red line, artificially linked to each other by history but equally artificially held off from the great magnet that lies to the south. As with many other federal states, Canada's economy needs action to bind it together, left to itself it will fall apart. Growth requires investment, and the investible funds are available in great quantity. But look where they come from. An economy whose investment comes preponderantly from a foreign country needs special guidance or direction. If it aims at growth and yet wishes to preserve its independence, it has a tough job.

Unfortunately these contentions carry little persuasion. First, take the experience of other countries. The evidence does not show that the Monnet Plan was the cause of causes of the recent splendid performance of the French economy. What the Monnet Plan did was to cause a great investment in basic industries; and so when the devaluation of the franc and the Rueff reforms of 1958 put French costs in a good competitive posture, the basic industries were well equipped to jump to it and help propel the economy forward. But the Monnet Plan started in 1947 and until 1958 the French economy was not in good shape. Now the essence of true planning is co-ordination. If the Monnet Plan was truly effective in this sense it would have shed brilliance on the French economy long before 1958. To spend money on steel, transport, and power may be good, but it does not amount to planning. And it may not even be good; it may only mean that you have, say, abundant power and scarce bread.

Of course the Monnet Plan has the appearance of true planning. It goes through the most intricate motions of co-ordination. The Commissariat au Plan makes elaborate computations and the numerous commissions for individual industries engage in a great deal of discussion. But the questions are: first, has this really determined the pattern of production in France, and secondly, has it really produced a co-ordination which would not otherwise have been there? In my opinion the answer to the first question is no, except in the cases of those large industries where public money has been available for investment, and to the second question an even less qualified no. The discussions in the commissions have produced some insights which would not have been there otherwise, but how can they be said really to have co-ordinated things so that a shift in, say the figure of output for one industry has been translated into a planned consequential change in the figures for other industries? The presence of labour representatives in the commissions would itself mean that the really vital decisions of the firms concerned could not be taken there. Hence, I do not believe that there has been much real planning behind the façade of the Monnet Plan.

In Britain we have decided that we too must do a Monnet *cum* Rueff exercise. And strangely enough, I believe that we have a very good chance of hitting our target of 4 per cent compound annual growth by 1966. That is because our economy now happens to be in good shape, which in itself is largely due to the steadfastness of our government in refusing to make growth *the* economic objective in the past, despite the siren voices of the planners! I know of no evidence that our NEDDY men know how to solve the extremely perplexing problems of producing a logical—as distinct from a hit-and-miss—co-ordination of the output of shoes, ships, sealing-wax, and the rest. As for NICKY, it cannot be called a planner at all. Its purpose is to make recommendations in particular cases of wage disputes which will keep the rate of increase of wages in parallel with that of productivity. There are perplexing analytical problems here which were not solved by the Cohen Council, and that was intellectually a far better equipped body than NICKY. Originally it was hoped that NICKY would produce wage-planning on the Dutch-Swedish model, but as the T.U.C. has rejected the whole idea (and who could have expected that it would not?) that door is closed.

The cases of the Netherlands, Italy, and Japan are not examples of planning at all on the definition which I have adopted. First consider the Dutch exercises, which in skill and sophistication lead the field. On the one hand the Dutch have established a central initiative for the determination of wages (the wage-planning to which I have referred above), and this bears the true impress of planning, *but only for what amounts to one of the determinants of the level of economic activity*, highly important though it is. When it comes to the "planning" of the whole economy, the Dutch have produced a highly elaborate system of forecasting but not a system for the application of the forecasts. Forecasting on its own does not amount to planning.

The Italian and the Japanese "plans" for the whole economy equally turn out to be exercises in forecasting and target-making, but not for practical application. Both the Italians and the Japanese have hit some splendid targets, but not because any planners set them up. In addition the Italians have, of course, their "plan" for the south. This, it is true, is not a mere affair of the drawing board; billions of lire have already been spent on applying it. But its essence is the channelling, to some extent the dragooning, of funds for investment in the south. Not merely is this not planning for what I would mean by "a substantial part of the Italian economy," for such a part could hardly exclude Lombardy and Piedmont; it is not even planning for the whole economy of the south, for there are numerous elements in the economy of the south which do not enter into the calculations governing the state-directed southern investment and expenditure. If one were to accept state intervention into such a part of the economy as planning, then the concept of planning would become diffuse and unmanageable, for the number of types of state intervention into parts of the economy is legion. Nor, for that matter, would the record of such state intervention be encouraging for the champions of planning.

But, you may protest, is it right to dismiss forecasting, where it attempts to cover substantially the whole economy, from the field of planning? Even if the forecasts are not applied, will they not have an influence on government policy and in particular on its budgeting? Yes, no doubt they will or may, but this does not turn them into a plan. If it did, it could be said that we in Britain have practised economic planning continuously since 1941 when, under the influence of Keynes, our budget first became based on an annual forecast of the quantitative performance of the economy (an exercise which, incidentally, has never been conspicuously accurate).

For these reasons I suggest that in considering the record of other countries one should put the Netherlands, Italy, and Japan in the camp of those countries, of which Western Germany is the most conspicuous example, which have achieved outstanding success without, not with, economic planning. On this view the experience of other countries generally would not support a case for a Canadian plan.

How about the second argument? The market fails in practice to do the job of co-ordination and so the state must do it. This is a pretty well-beaten field of disputation. I need only say that in the first place the apparent failures of the market can nearly all be attributed extremely persuasively to cross-grained and ill-conceived interferences with it by the state; and in the second place there is absolutely no evidence that, if you clothe even the wisest men with state power, they will know how to co-ordinate the myriads of transactions and relationships which make up a modern economy as well as, not to mention better than, the market. Of course the kind of co-ordination which results from the manipulations of monetary policy, tariff policy, and fiscal policy is another matter. This is hard enough in all conscience, but it is possibly manageable. At any rate it has to be managed, which means that it is best to let the state get on with these jobs and show that it can manage them before considering more grand assignments.

Finally there is the argument founded on the special features of the Canadian economy. These result from the choice by the Canadian people of certain non-economic objectives. They have chosen—and I hope the verdict of history will be that they have chosen aright—a particular political destiny. In a world of free trade, of an almost automatic gold standard, and of minimal economic functions for the state, this would have made little economic difference. But in a world where monetary, fiscal, and tariff policies are bound to have a large impact, the political shape of Canada produces something like an economic monstrosity. I concede, therefore that the Canadian economy needs some management, and pretty skilled management at that. But management is not the same as planning in the sense I have adopted. Once again one is forced back to the conclusion that the Canadian government has plenty to do in its existing fields of operation; that in fact it would do better if it did even less than it does; that it would be more successful, for example, if it had not given itself the difficult task of managing its monetary system under a regime of fixed exchange rates, and if it gave the market more scope by relying less on tariffs as an instrument of policy. My conclusion is that in the special features of the Canadian situation there is no ground for the belief that more power, more dictation, and more concerted action in Ottawa is what is needed.

But perhaps my definition of planning is unsatisfactory after all. The economic tasks of the modern democratic state are heavy enough. If they were discharged with more coherence, more foresight, and more understanding of the interrelations of things, that too, as I have suggested at the beginning of this paper, might be called a plan! In that sense, but in my opinion in that sense only, Canada needs a plan, as do we all.

Harry G. Johnson

Planning of the type currently practised in some countries might even retard economic growth. . . .

In recent years, a country's rate of economic growth has become a measure of its economic performance widely used in international comparisons, and an object of policy for its government. In the United States and Canada the rate of economic growth in the past five years has been much less than it was earlier in the post-war period, and well below the average rate of growth of continental Europe. Concern over this relatively poor performance, and its implications for North America's political and economic power in the world, has converted a number of eminent people in the two countries to the view that what is needed is some kind of economic planning. This view is reinforced, not entirely logically, by the observation that in some of the fast-growing European countries—notably France—economic planning is the established practice. In some quarters in Canada, indeed, planning has come to be recommended as the magic solution to all the country's problems, especially the problem of growth.

Before one goes overboard for economic planning, however, it is necessary to consider what are the sources of economic growth, and how planning might be expected to accelerate growth. Essentially, the argument for planning as a means to growth is that planning will both increase the rate of investment, and make investment more efficient. The crucial question, therefore, is how much more investment, and more efficient investment, can contribute to growth. The answer depends on how important investment is as a source of growth. And the results of the research on the sources of growth that has been steadily accumulating over the past decade strongly indicate that investment—the accumulation of capital—is not a major source of growth.

The term "economic growth" is sometimes used to mean growth of total income (gross national product) and sometimes growth of income per head; the former is the more relevant for national economic strength, the latter for individual economic welfare. Whichever definition is used, the rate of growth needs to be measured over a fairly long period of time, as otherwise the long-term factors will be swamped by the influence of the business cycle—any country can show a phenomenal rate of growth over a year or two, if bad luck or mismanagement enables it to start from a severe enough depression.

Most of the research on the sources of economic growth completed so far has been concerned with the growth of the American economy. The basic outline of such research has been to assume that the growth of national income is due to three factors—growth of the working population, accumulation of capital, and a residual factor labelled "technical change"—and to isolate the relative importance of these factors by econometric techniques. The results have invariably assigned a very small part of growth to capital accumulation and a very large part to the residual category of technical change. Since the residual category amounts to a confession of ignorance, more recent work has attempted to account for the residue by other factors not included in the quantities of labour and capital. Among such factors, those that have received most attention are improvements in the quality of labour and machinery. Improvements in the quality of labour are identified with formal education and in-plant training, and measured by the value of the stock of education or "human capital"; improvements in the quality of machinery and other productive inputs are measured by changes in the cost of obtaining a standardized performance. Other work has concentrated on the importance of shifts of labour and capital from less productive to more productive sectors of the economy, which increase the efficiency with which labour and capital are used.

The most comprehensive analysis of the sources of economic growth in the United States is contained in a Committee for Economic Development study by Edward F. Denison, published under that title. Denison finds that 68 per cent of the U.S. growth of real national income from 1928 to 1957 is accounted for by increased inputs into production, and 32 per cent is accounted for by increased output per unit of input. Of the 68 per cent due to increased inputs, 54 points represents increased labour and the remainder increased capital; of the 54 points due to increased labour, 27 points are due to increased labour hours, 23 to increased education, and 4 to increased experience and better utilization of women workers. Of the 32 per cent due to increased output per unit of input, 20 are due to the advance of knowledge, 11 to economies of scale, and 3 to reduced waste of labour in agriculture and the shift from agriculture to industry, 2 points being subtracted by increased restrictions on efficient use of resources. Denison finds that only 15 per cent of the total increase in U.S. real national income, and only 9 per cent of the increase in real national income per person employed, is attributable to increased capital; and he reckons that to increase the growth rate between 1960 and 1980 by $\frac{1}{10}$ per cent would require an increase of annual private net investment by one-quarter. The same increase in the growth rate, he calculates, could be attained by increasing the standard work week by about an hour, or reducing by 2⅔ years the lag of average production practices behind the best known.

The results of these studies of U.S. growth all suggest that capital accumulation is not a very important contributor to growth, and that a substantial increase in the rate of investment would have a relatively insignificant effect on the growth rate. Various comparative studies of the relation between investment and growth in different countries also suggest that there is no close causal connection between investment and growth. An O.E.C.D. study published last autumn, for example, showed that there is no close connection between investment rates and growth rates in Europe because the efficiency of investment varies widely between countries. Sweden, investing 21 per cent of gross domestic product, had a low rate of growth while France, investing 16 per cent of gross domestic product, had a high rate of growth, the difference being due to a substantial difference in the additional output obtained per unit of investment. Incidentally, the efficiency of investment was highest in Germany, not France; the study attributes Germany's superior investment efficiency to the innovation-mindedness of German industry, the keenness of competition in the domestic market, and the greater dominance of technical men in investment decision-making.

All of these studies, therefore, suggest that the main sources of economic growth lie beyond the scope of national planning of investment, and that the key factors relate to the development and application of knowledge. It is conceivable that a type of planning could be developed that would concentrate on these factors, but it would be a different type of planning from economic planning as now practised. Planning of the type currently practised in some countries might even retard growth, by removing the stimulus to innovation that competition in the market now provides.

H. Scott Gordon

The basic ideas of economic planning nowadays are integration and co-ordination rather than planning as such.

Everybody plans. Consumers plan how to spend their budgets: how to provide for their families' immediate needs for such things as food and clothing; how to provide for needs that involve longer-term decisions, such as housing; how to provide for needs that are at present only prospective, such as retirement. Businessmen are nothing if not planners. Production schedules, marketing programmes, investment projections—what business executive does not spend most of his time in bondage to these plans, constructing them, revising them, executing them? Even governments plan, despite the fact that their life expectancy is much shorter than a large corporation's or even that of a head of a household.

Planning is something everyone does who has any sense of tomorrow. A bum doesn't plan ahead; that is what makes him a bum. A condemned prisoner in his death cell doesn't plan ahead—except possibly by means of prayer. The rest of us are planning all the time. The sense of the future is more with us than the past, or even the present. Foresight is more sought after than hindsight. History is only of academic interest; *prediction*—there's the real practical stuff.

When we talk about economic planning nowadays, and the functions of France's Commissariat and Britain's NEDDY and Canada's own NEDDY to come, we are not fundamentally considering an increase in the amount of planning. These institutions have not come into being because there has been too little thought about the future; they are not really efforts to increase the average "telescopic capacity" of the French or the British or ourselves. The innovation is more fundamentally qualitative than quantitative. The basic ideas are *integration* and *co-ordination* rather than planning as such. What these institutions are really supposed to do is to integrate the planning that goes on all over the economy; to put it all together to see if the thing as a whole makes economic sense, and to see if it makes the kind of economic sense we want in terms of the economic and social objectives we set for society.

This type of planning, which we might call Integrative Planning in order to display its most basic characteristic, is not being instituted and advocated today because without it the economic process would be a chaos of independent and unrelated plans and actions. After all, that is precisely what the price system is supposed to do. The "discord" which Alexander Pope said was really "harmony not understood" *is* understood by anyone who has studied the economic theory of the price system. Even the deep pink planners, among the economists at least, acknowledge that there is a wide area of economic activity where the automatic integrating of the price system does better than a Commissariat or a NEDDY.

But all is not perfect harmony under the price system. In the area of capital investment expenditures, there are particularly strong reasons for doubting whether the many independent plans of businesses and governments will add up to the right amounts and be distributed in even an approximately satisfactory way. Integrative planning has the task of discovering these contemplated disharmonies before the individual policies are translated into action, and of advising the federal government concerning the means that might be employed to correct them. To the orthodox techniques of monetary policy and fiscal policy others will probably have to be added to persuade, induce (and we might even add "require," *sotto voce*) the private plans of private business to undergo whatever changes are necessary to integrate these plans into a desirable coherence.

In Canada, in addition, we will face some problems that other countries like France and Britain do not know. Here, we will have to do special things to co-ordinate the various plans for public as well as private investment, for we do not have government in Canada; we have government*s*, plural.

The areas where public investment in the creation of social capital are most needed in Canada are the responsibilities of the provinces and of their creatures, the municipalities. The integration of the public investment programmes of ten provincial and hundreds of municipal governments with that of the federal government will be much harder to do than to wish for. It will take a great deal of skill on the part of public administrators, plus unaccustomed long-sightedness on the part of politicians, to restrain the British North America Act from preventing the Canadian economy from being dragged into the modern world.

R. V. Yohe

In many aspects the economic activities of a nation may be pursued in much the same way that businesses are operated.

I am a strong proponent of the theory that many of the economic phases of government, whether that government is federal or provincial, parliamentarian or republican, can be responsive to the precepts and methods that have proved to be most successful in the operation of a business, be it manufacturing, service, or extractive in type.

Admittedly this is an old theme that has been worked over orally and about as completely as a holiday turkey until only the bare bones are left. Note that I said orally, for that is about as far as it has got. Anytime anyone tries to inject into government the practical and necessary procedures of efficiency, cost reduction, and production planning used by business, he runs afoul of so many political limitations that he often gives up in despair—and I might add, disgust. Despite the lip service given to the magnificent Hoover *Report*, it has been very inadequately implemented even to this day. I predict that the Glassco *Report* in Canada will have a similar fate. I doubt that there is a party in Canada with the courage or the political integrity to implement it to the degree that it should be implemented. Certainly the Democrats and the Republicans in the United States had their opportunities and came up wanting.

In business, efficiency and all of its corollaries are forced on each operative by competition. No president of a corporation ever enhanced his reputation with his stockholders by managing his company into bankruptcy. Yet, time after time, politicians in democracy everywhere get themselves elected to office by advocating measures which, when and if enacted, would lead to national circumstances that are financially at odds with the long-run best interests of the country. I have yet to hear a politician say that he could not honestly support an idea more costly than the nation could bear if he felt that by supporting it votes would be gained that would be lost to him if he took a contrary non-supporting position. It is no compliment to a democratic electorate that continues to condone such perfidy.

As I have indicated, businesses are forced to be competitive in quality, service, and price if they expect to remain in the market-place. A possible exception might be a company that had a proprietary product of considerable demand with no competition. Such a situation usually breeds complacency and carelessness, and eventually the owner wakes up some fine morning to find that someone has discovered a satisfactory substitute for his product at a lower price.

A company that makes products which are widely used, but also manufactured and sold competitively, looks continuously to increased productivity, improved equipment, better methods, and improved quality at lower costs. It also continuously explores its markets for expansion and plans new ways of satisfying consumer needs with lower distribution costs.

In the competitive nature of things today, the similarity between whole nations and a manufacturer in a multi-product business seems obvious. I believe there is a strong case for the contention that in many aspects the economic activities of a nation may be pursued in much the same way that businesses are operated.

To illustrate my point, permit me to describe an actual case history of a company in Canada, the circumstance in which that company found itself being remarkably similar to the economic circumstances in which Canada finds itself. I ask that you allow your imagination freely to substitute Canada and Canadian circumstances to this case history as I proceed with my description. As I stated, the story is true, but names have been changed in order to protect next of kin!

The company I have in mind manufactures and sells a wide variety of products, most of which were satisfactorily profitable but over half of its ouput is in one classification of product. This high volume product is sold in a very competitive market. The company had been experiencing a severe quality problem with this product, brought on by its own carelessness coupled with inadequate and somewhat obsolete manufacturing equipment. Manufacturing costs were high and, in a highly price-competitive market, profits had deteriorated badly. The company accountably had steadily lost industry position in this product line. In essence, such was the situation that the company—which we shall call the XYZ Corporation—found itself in a very few years ago.

The steps that were taken were as follows:

1. A tremendous technical effort was begun to return the product to a state of quality equivalent to, or better than competition. This effort was successful in about one year's time, even with the somewhat obsolete facilities.

2. Then, since it was apparent that costs of manufacture necessary to obtain a satisfactory profit, if any at all, were impossible in the old plant, steps were taken to design and erect a multi-million-dollar, completely new facility, modern in every way known to the industry, and so designed as to have the lowest manufacturing cost for the product in question in Canada. The capacity of the new plant was to be equivalent only to an industry position in a 1955 expanded market. Even so, this was 60 per cent greater capacity in units than the old plant.

The plant took nearly two years to build. It is now in operation.

3. Finally, eighteen months prior to the new plant completion, in recognition of the fact that the XYZ Corporation's marketing activities were about as obsolete as its production facilities, and that the production capacity of the new plant had to be realized in sales, a complete reorganization of the marketing organization was called for.

The following excerpts are from the brief of the plan of reorganization.

XYZ CORPORATION LIMITED

A PLAN FOR MARKET ORIENTED MANAGEMENT

A review of immediate past sales and profits of XYZ Corporation Limited provides ample evidence that, because of organization, personnel, product, and perhaps some of each, the Company has been unable to cope with problems of the market. Even further, a review of the past several years demonstrates that in spite of some successes and some growth there is no real evidence that the company has kept pace with the potential of the total Canadian market and has, in some categories, lost considerable ground.

It cannot be honestly said that the whole fault has been in marketing, although it is certainly true that marketing methods have been product oriented instead of market oriented. It is true that in some products, particularly in the smaller area of special products in which we participate, our marketing methods and our manufacturing have been reasonably successful. It is, however, painfully evident that our main product quality problems and the selling procedures associated with them have contributed to slow growth, if any, and to poor profits.

Since a quality product, acceptable to the buyer of our main product, is a must before a marketing plan of any kind would have any possible chance of success, steps have been taken to insure that improvements are made in its manufacture, using all technical facilities in the corporation available to Canada for this purpose. In addition, a new manufacturing plant is under construction which will incorporate as many of the advanced techniques associated with such manufacture as is possible to obtain in a plant of the size contemplated. The end result will be higher quality at lower costs.

We have every reason to believe that our products in the future will be of such quality as to be competitive or better in the Canadian market. We believe that our manufacturing organization and personnel are capable of providing the talents necessary to operate our facilities to best advantage, cost- and quality-wise.

The over-all task, therefore, is that of disposing of the products from our manufacturing facilities profitably in an expanding, highly competitive market. We do not believe we are now organized, staffed or oriented market-wise to accomplish this task. This presentation submits a reorganization of functions and responsibilities for all of XYZ Corporation, recommends certain marketing procedural changes, suggests certain job eliminations and additions and suggests further that, through the combination of all of these, a proper climate will be established for making XYZ Corporation the profitable, growth company, that it must become.

THE PLAN

It will be assumed in this presentation that the marketing concept is an accepted tenet and applicable to the broad problems of XYZ Corporation, the solutions for which this plan is designed to help achieve. Actually marketing is rather difficult to define in concrete terms although many facets of it lend themselves to concrete definition. Broadly speaking, marketing relates a whole business to the point of view of the customer, to his demands, and to the satisfaction of these demands. Specifically, however, marketing, or at least the concept of it as generally accepted, provides for full and detailed coordination of a wide variety of functions, each capable of description and defined accountability.

After the establishment of objectives by management, creation of policies, and preparation of long range plans which are consonant with those objectives and policies, it is possible to organize a company into areas of responsibility and action so as to give specific implementation to the marketing concept.

It is to this purpose that this proposal is directed. It must be conceded at this point that any plan will only be successful to the degree that management direction and basic personnel assignments are of the caliber necessary for success.

XYZ Corporation is not large enough to warrant divisionalization on a single product basis or on a segment basis. Therefore, this plan will endeavour to recommend an organized approach to marketing for the total company. In some areas consolidation of like and similar functions will be made in the interests of intensification and direction, solicitation, or economy. In all cases it is expected that penetration of the market will be enhanced rather than retarded, particularly if auxiliary functions of the marketing organization operate according to the definition of these functions.

I present this to illustrate a planned approach to the illness of an individual company. I have omitted the reorganization details and the problems of financing a multi-million-dollar expenditure. I have not mentioned the heartburn that accompanies the digestion of new personnel and new methods, the personnel problems that ensue when people are rudely rooted out of their ruts of routine, and the pains that accompany the start-up of a new plant. It would be pleasant to report that all the ideals envisioned in the reorganization plan had been realized. I do understand, however, that the XYZ Corporation set a new over-all sales record in 1962 and that its profitable items became more so, even although the product which actuated all of this transformation, while contributing the highest sales volume for many years, still continues to be unprofitable. However, the full benefits from the new plant are yet to come; and the test of the conversion to a marketing approach has only been partially completed and proven out.

You perhaps have followed my suggestion that economic Canada be substituted for the XYZ Corporation in this case history. You have, perhaps, noted the similarity between Canada and XYZ Corporation in competitive areas of costs and selling prices. You noted that borrowing of money was necessary to finance capital improvement; that technical improvement was a must in order to obtain product quality to satisfy consumer demand and meet competitive circumstances; that the product to be manufactured must be designed to customer needs and wants.

While I spent some time on a plan of reorganization, with emphasis on the planning of marketing, I did not elaborate on the actual planning, product by product and segment by segment, in the XYZ Corporation since reorganization. What is significant is that detailed plans were actually laid out during the last eighteen months in each of these areas, not only for the near future but on a five-year basis. These plans analysed the market for each product, established goals of anticipated sales, and elaborated on the methods by which these goals were to be achieved.

It is reassuring to report that in every area, including the most troublesome one, outstanding achievement is already occurring.

And now, to indicate further the rather apt similarity between the economic aspects of a nation and those of a business, let me suggest that:

1. The exports of a nation may be likened to the sales of a single multi-product manufacturer with all of the aspects of good marketing practices, such as I have described, applying to both.

2. The important area of imports of a nation may be likened to the purchase of materials by a company from outside suppliers.

3. Taxes on the businesses and people of a country are analogous to the non-productive costs of running a business.

4. Importation of capital resembles bank borrowing.

And as I have said in previous discussions on this similarity, knowing when to wield taxing authority or relax it—establish subsidies or remove them—resort to price supports or not—reach co-operative agreements with other nations—all these and more have counterparts in the running of a business; they are of great significance in the running of a nation. All are designed to create a profit for a nation: a profit which is a better standard of living for its people at a rate of improvement which does not generate localized excess burdens or inhibit economic development in any area.

The genius that is management, although certainly all management is not so gifted, knows when to expand to satisfy a profitable market, when to reduce costs when it is necessary to do so to be competitive, when to reduce prices to achieve greater sales volume at a profit when to increase prices if income is not providing an adequate return on capital investment. Is it too much to hope that equivalent genius might be found in government for the establishment of policies and plans for the satisfactory accomplishment of corresponding elements in the conduct of a nation?

A multi-product company accurately indicates changing consumer tastes through marketing research. A nation studies its foreign markets thoroughly and guides its productive talents towards these markets. A manufacturing company recognizes the need for and dramatizes high quality in its products. A nation makes sure that its exports are of the kind, the quality, and the design to meet the needs and demands of its export customers. These, and all the other precepts of modern marketing methods are applicable not only in the relations of one country with another but in internal affairs as well. Above all, however, a plan must be established which clearly defines objectives and develops a time-table for accomplishment. The plan itself should call for constant reappraisal and change as circumstances change. The application of sound marketing principles to all aspects of Canada's trade position, and to her position as a competitive, free enterprise nation in an alliance of free nations is a thoughtful, possible solution to the circumstances in which she finds herself.

The time has probably come when Canada should depart from the "policy" laid down by Sir John A. Macdonald and to which Canada has tried to adhere since the time of Confederation. This does not mean that there should be no policy. Quite the contrary: it is really within the area of policy-making that Canada is floundering at the moment. There are so many conflicting forces at work in the economy, so many divergent views, so much emotion, that a firm, clear, and definite policy, designed to make the implementation of a comprehensive plan for Canada's internal and external trading activities workable, is almost impossible to prepare, much less carry out.

Try as you will, it is rarely possible to dissociate the political aspects of a country from its economic aspects, particularly now in Canada.

Even the European Common Market is finding it necessary to face up to this problem in the broad context of its internal economic associations.

A policy or policies there should be, however, accompanied by well-defined objectives for which plans are drawn for achievement. None of these should be static. They should be co-operatively developed by and with the understanding, if not always the complete approbation of all elements—labour, management, government. They should be designed to accelerate the effective functioning of the total economy and, relating them to my earlier simile, be designed to create a profit for the nation. This profit, naturally, is an improved standard of living for the whole population.

The success of the planning effort will be dependent on the voluntary support of labour and management. This support would most likely be forthcoming in direct proportion to the enthusiastic participation of these two elements of modern economic society in the planning process.

A note of warning should be sounded here. If we want to avoid the hazards of government domination in the planning process, and these hazards are many, then a unified front of management and labour *vis-à-vis* government should be established to make sure that national programming is kept on an indicative basis. Permitting government to develop plans and subsequently endowing it with power to force compliance to them could lead to the very characteristics that we decry in totalitarian economies.

Other than in the area of productivity, the most fruitful area of management-labour co-operation could be a common policing of the planning process for the purpose of preserving free enterprise and the capitalistic system. Such a common endeavour would in no way abrogate the rights of both management and labour to settle their mutual problems without government intervention. In fact such intervention is not in keeping with our way of doing things. Labour-management problems should be resolved at their own levels.

With these warnings and with safeguards properly implemented, I would say almost categorically that Canada does need planning and could profit from the procedures of indicative programming. I would certainly not advocate the rigidity of execution that a corporation can apply to its planning processes but if centralized planning is used to provide the atmosphere for the total economy of a country, and decentralized planning, industry by industry, company by company, is used for the purpose of furthering growth of the various sectors in it, then the planning process could be of great benefit to Canada. Proper and complete communication and understanding of the objectives of the nation would undoubtedly in a large measure influence the planning of the various sectors and control their possible excesses. Even some excesses would be a small price to pay in order to retain the freedom of action so desirable in our democratic way of life.

I was a member of the Mission to Europe sponsored by the productivity Council of Canada. I will not attempt any description of the mission itself, its objectives, activities, or conclusions. These are all available in the *Report* of the mission. We explored, among many other things, the degree to which planning or indicative programming, as most countries in Western Europe like to call it, had contributed to the economic successes of the six countries visited. We found an extreme variation in the way national planning was implemented, varying from the sophisticated French marketing-type approach to the economic *laissez-faire* approach (where the market itself dictates the end result) of Germany.

The primary objectives of full employment, healthy balance of payments and trade, price stability, and a rising standard of living were common to all six countries. The methods used by individual countries varied because of economic circumstance, rehabilitation needs, dependence on export, and the national character of the people. After recognizing that each country had varying degrees of social, political, and cultural development within itself, it was somewhat surprising to find that all were developing their planning on a common pattern, namely, that competitive circumstances and other market influences were the controlling factors in the utilization of people and productive facilities. As would be the case in any good marketing organization, these single countries then endeavoured to use these primary factors effectively for the common good of the country itself. While the degree of success varied from country to country, so also did the degree of success vary from company to company within each country. An interesting sidelight, and related to productivity, rationalization, and industry co-operation, was the fact that lack of success by individual companies within industries, and indeed by whole industries, was intolerable and was treated appropriately. This is a whole subject in itself.

It may be concluded that planning or indicative programming has demonstrative merit in the successful functioning of a business and preliminary proof has been brought forward that it has merit in the economic aspects of whole countries. While it remains to be seen whether whole populations may become so intoxicated with success that they may also, in that intoxication, become so careless in policing the use of planning that they lose their economic freedoms, nevertheless, this hazard may have to be faced if any single nation is to remain a factor in a world-wide competitive economy.

George F. Bain

There are two kinds of economic planning. One sort is the planning of final demands and the other sort is the planning of total output.

The main thing to be realized is that there are few instances of planning which are successful on a national scale. Planning requires that many individual units of decision-making give up some of their ability to make free choices. The corollary is that new economic units are formed to assume the responsibility of decision-making for sub-units of the economy. Thus national planning involves both the surrender of a certain amount of freedom and the creation of a system of more centralized decision-making.

There are, basically, two kinds of planning. One sort is the planning of final demands and the other sort is the planning of industry output or, from the national point of view, the planning of total output. While it can be argued that these two kinds of planning are really two sides of the same coin, there are great differences in the philosophy underlying them. In one the doctrine of consumers' choice is paramount; in the other the state—the general welfare—is supreme.

In Western countries a national economic plan tries to achieve a given level of final demand. These levels of final demand are usually derived from a forecast of desired growth or some view of how much consumption, investment, exports, and so forth, is required by the economy in order to achieve, say, full employment. Modern technique takes the level of final demand and, using certain technical relationships between inputs and outputs and various industry and cost and price data, identifies appropriate levels of total output in various sectors of the economy. So a target level of consumption for next year can be translated by planners into required levels of output in the automobile industry, in the clothing industry and in the general service industry sectors, and so on, which are consistent with the desired level of total consumer demand.

In the West, the next step in the plan is to create proper incentives in order to induce attainment of the future final demand level of consumption. Western planners also attempt to induce appropriate responses of output in various industries via manipulation of taxes, interest rates, and so on, so that output in the consumer goods industries will become consistent with the over-all final demand assumed by the plan.

In the Russian, or fully socialist economies, planning takes only a somewhat different form. The achievement of certain levels of total output in various industries, such as the electrical industry or the steel industry, is in itself considered to be an appropriate goal. Planning in socialist economies therefore tends to proceed from the output side. Political choices are made about the appropriate output, or growth, to be realized in steel, clothing, electricity, consumer goods industries, and so on, in the belief (one supposes) that high growth rates in basic industries imply an over-all buoyant growth in the total economy.[1]

The Soviet planners, having been given these output figures for industry, set up what they call a material balance for the economy, and this material balance estimate is checked to see that the total output in the various industries can be absorbed by other industries and, eventually, by the final consumption sectors. Modern techniques, similar to those used in the West, can be used by the Soviets to make an internally consistent plan.

In general, the two kinds of basic planning—the planning of final demands and the planning of industry or total output—approach the same ends. The Soviets are finding, now that their planning process is coming to depend more and more on an understanding and awareness of the marginal nature of the choices facing them and on the importance of relative prices (which tend to divert resources along non-technological lines), that the planning process requires a new approach. The Soviets are, thus, coming more and more to the conclusion that their economy can plan effectively only by using many of the incentives that the West has used. Here in the West, I think that we are coming to realize that the attempt to plan for final demand levels is not the most precise way in which planning can proceed. We are becoming less willing than before to put up with slow growth and structural unemployment, and more willing to specify industry output goals.

[1]Businessmen in the West, generally speaking, tend to plan more along the lines of socialist planning than along the lines of non-socialist planning. That is, the firm's output is considered to be a desirable goal and, incidental to this, sales forces and advertising and distribution facilities are set up in an attempt to dispose of the desired level of total output. It is reasoned by the firm, not always correctly, that the highest output is the most desirable goal. Most corporation businessmen would not agree that to be small and profitable is better than to be large and, perhaps, less profitable in terms of rate of return on capital. The maximization of sales and output becomes a firm's goal. Monument building in business is probably a result of this emphasis on maximizing total output within the firm.

Errors in planning will always occur. In Western economies the errors in planning are, generally speaking, revealed in under-employment, in the existence of the trade cycle, in the existence of unemployment, and in the misallocation of resources. In Soviet economies, errors in planning are not necessarily revealed in unemployment but they are revealed in a misallocation of resources and, therefore in the appearance of surpluses or shortages and in the maldistribution of goods within the economy.

It seems, too, that in both the Western and the Soviet economies, planning for the agricultural sector is neither efficient, nor effective, nor capable of being accomplished. The Soviet agricultural planning problem is that total output cannot be increased by the planning system that exists today. Therefore, the Soviets are tending, more and more, to insert into their plans the type of economic incentive which exists in the West. This will, inevitably, spill over into the industrial sector and make their economy more like ours. In the West, our planning for agriculture has often proceeded along lines that the Soviets would not find strange: that is, the creation of a plan for total output or for limiting total output in the agricultural sector. The problem in the West has been that we have too many surpluses in agriculture. The incentives are too attractive, and the ability to restrict total output is overcome by technological advances. Planning in the agricultural sector does not seem possible in the present state of the art. On the whole it seems more moral to try to have surpluses than to have shortages—but this is not an economic problem, it is a theological one.

From what I have said it must not be implied that I believe that the planning of national economies can be particularly efficiently accomplished. I think that, as countries become more developed, the goals of planning become less precise and more general, and, as between the West and Russia, more similar. The root of the problem, particularly for a federal state such as Canada, is to achieve co-operation in planning between the various levels of government, and to recognize that the plan is basically one which attempts to achieve an increment over the average rate of growth achievable without planning. Another aim might be to eliminate the business cycle, although concentration on this objective seems to me to be unrealistic in an open economy.

In order to achieve an increment in the average rate of growth which we are now realizing, it cannot be said that economic planning can accomplish very much. In recent studies of the U.S. economy, Mr. E. F. Denison ("The Lagging U.S. Growth Rate," *American Economic*

51

Review, May 1962, p. 67 ff.) has suggested that in order to increase the growth rate by one per cent per annum over an existing rate, $^{82}/_{100}$ of this increase (i.e., .82 of the one percentage point) will be realized by:

an increase in knowledge + an increase in the level of education + a more rapid spread of modern business practices	.14 per annum
longer working hours by the labour force	.28 per annum
larger immigration	.20 per annum
increased capital input	.20 per annum
	.82 per annum

All other sorts of changes, such as the elimination of structural unemployment, freer international trade, the elimination of labour restrictions, consolidation of enterprises, and so on, amount to an increase of only $^{18}/_{100}$ of the extra per cent per annum increase in growth.

From this it seems clearly indicated that economic planning can mainly affect only the capital input of an economy. This item gives only a small impetus to increased growth. More capital input implies greater saving and, thus, either an autonomous change in consumption propensities or the creation of government surpluses. The problem is complicated, in our open economy, because we no longer can assume that our monetary policy can be independent, tied as it is to the U.S. economy.

Economic planning must, therefore, rely upon the tax system (fiscal policy) or upon a greater degree of state direction to achieve the increased capital expenditure necessary for a more rapid rate of growth. So we come up against the political aspects of a democratic, federal state. Only by co-operative long-run planning at the government level—the planning of taxation incentives and disincentives; the planning of provincial, municipal, and federal expenditure over a period of years; the creation of politically stable plans—will Canada see its growth rate influenced to any great degree by economic planning.

But Denison's data, until something else comes along, also indicates that more immigration and all-out support for research and education will probably yield as much, in terms of growth, as economic planning.

So long as the Canadian people will put up with an average level of unemployment of nearly 11 per cent (February, 1961) and local unemployment pockets of over 20 per cent, we should not bother too much about trying to reduce cyclical swings in employment but, rather, concentrate on reducing average unemployment over the cycle by stimulating the rate of growth.

PART III

What Kind of Planning for Canada?

Interdependence in modern economic life necessitates the extension of planning once it has been started. . . . Any large rapid extension of machinery (for economic planning) with vague notions as to its character and effects would undoubtedly have serious consequences. But thorough study, careful integration, ample provisions for flexibility, and careful adjusted relationships to existing machinery with a view to capitalizing available economic skill and intelligence should provide a base for a structure which can be gradually improved as experience is gained from its operations and effects.

HAROLD A. INNIS*

*From *Canadian Problems: As Seen by Twenty Outstanding Men of Canada*, Toronto, Oxford University Press, 1933, pp. 69–90.

Arthur J. R. Smith*

What can we learn that is of relevance for Canada from the experience of other democratic, industrially advanced nations which have established some form of economic planning organization?

A few years ago it would have been difficult to conceive of holding a conference in Canada on the question of whether Canada needed economic planning. At least, I suggest, it would have proved difficult to draw together a broad cross-section of business, labour, professional, and other people to discuss and debate this question seriously.

But attitudes and times have changed. Considerable interest has developed in Canada in economic planning. Nevertheless, at this Conference the counting and assessing of the pros and cons of economic planning did not turn out to be the chief labour at all. The main exercise was quite clearly that of attempting to define what kind of game economic planning might be, and in particular whether it should be a "barking" game or a "biting" game. A "barking" approach is one in which there would be a voice to explain or urge certain lines of economic development or policy. A "biting" approach is one in which there would be teeth to help to ensure the attainment of specified objectives.

Among some of the key questions which have come up are the following. What is economic planning? Why do we need economic planning? Who should do it? Whom will it influence? What organizational arrangements are appropriate? What methods and techniques could be usefully employed in planning? Who will control the economic planners? Is economic planning compatible with our democratic traditions and market economy? What can we learn that is of relevance for Canada from the experience of other democratic, industrially advanced nations which have established some form of economic planning organization?

Incidentally, on this last question there was a very general view among those who are well informed on foreign experience that it was not at all clear that economic planning abroad could be credited with

*From his Introductory Address, Plenary Session, February 10.

54

a key role in the attainment of high growth rates, low unemployment, and strong balance of payments positions.

On many of these questions, opinions at the Conference varied widely. A considerable number of people in the discussion groups were at least sceptical of any conceptions of planning which would go beyond what might be termed the "artichoke approach" to planning. The claim was made that with an increasingly complex economic and social system, it has become much more difficult to understand the possible consequences of, and interrelationships between, the different types of private and public policies and decisions. These people believe that it is therefore necessary, as with an artichoke, to do a great deal of peeling to get to the heart of economic issues. This points to a basic need—perhaps preferably within an existing government department rather than in a separate economic planning organization—for a special task force of competent analysts to appraise the consequences of different policy decisions, and perhaps even to project the probable pathway of a nation's economic development over a number of years.

Another approach was that in our increasingly complex system there may be a need for some form of economic planning to do two things: First, to develop greater policy co-ordination within the government as a basis for ensuring that there is consistency between government policies aimed at achieving national economic objectives. Second, to develop greater understanding between governments and the private sectors (as well as among the private sectors), so that different elements of decision-making do not work at cross purposes with each other. To some, however, these very limited approaches to what may be termed "economic planning" appeared to amount to little more than the application of intelligent thought and intelligent action to a country's economic problems and opportunities.

A potentially further-reaching approach is what might be called the "Yogi Bear" approach to economic planning, encompassing an advisory role for a national planning organization. In other words, planning should be able to tell government and business and other groups what the economy needs to eat for breakfast to get going and keep growing.

But a basic question remains to be answered. It is this: does a country have anything which can genuinely be called economic planning until it has a combination of three things: planners to suggest objectives; policies (including, if necessary "incentives" or "compulsions") to achieve these objectives; and constant reappraisal of targets and techniques to assure progress towards accepted goals?

Jacques Parizeau

Planning a foreign-controlled economy with a federal constitution is a challenge that can be met only after a drastic revolution has taken place in the minds of the people.

Economic planning belongs to the doctrines of several political parties and at the same time has become fashionable in the so-called leftist wing of public opinion. Largely because of such an affiliation, planning has sometimes acquired in this country the atmosphere and colour of a quasi-religious dogma. And it becomes very difficult to discuss it on the basis of its own merits.

In effect, I think one must say that planning is a technique and only a technique. One does not have to be in favour or against it, once and for all. The only yardstick by which planning must be judged is its efficiency and results in a given country and at a given time. Either it works or it does not. Of course there are many ways of planning an economy, some very rigid and compelling, others with much less rigidity and more adapted to the normal interplay of conflicting interests. Political convictions may well induce rejection of some forms of planning. But it should be realized that the various forms of planning are not irremediably linked to definite political regimes. The most precise and all-embracing form of planning known to the historians is not that of communist Russia, but that of the Inca Empire, or of the Jesuit Fathers in Paraguay, and a great deal of contemporary planning in France would not have been incompatible with the mercantilist ideas of Colbert and Turgot at the time of the monarchy. And the present efforts of French Canadians to elaborate some forms of a planned economy is a far cry from the system of control they knew under the French regime.

Even during the course of the nineteenth century, at a time when the government in Britain was geared towards increasing abstention in economic matters, the Canadian government played a considerable role in the growth and orientation of our economy that could easily have fitted into a plan if the word had been invented. The organization of water and rail transport in this country is largely the result of massive intervention of the state. The links that existed between settlement, transportation, and tariff policy are well known. Even provincial governments went so far as to prohibit, in the early years of this century, the export of pulpwood cut on Crown land (and at that time it was a major stroke), thus making it necessary to the newsprint industry to expand in this country. Only when the structural mainsprings of the Canadian economy had been put into position, did the state sit back and let the free interplay of private business take full charge of the development of the economy. In fact it was only at the beginning of this century that Canada did at last participate fully in what had become in industrial countries an economic dogma: that of the free enterprise system unhindered and unbridled at least as far as its participation in growth is concerned.

The refusal to plan that is derived from the doctrine of economic liberalism is a direct result of the industrial revolution itself. It is, historically, well limited in time. The basis of the system is the market, a market where adjustments are possible between fairly small economic agents that react individually to the market but cannot influence it individually to any great extent. The system is under the guidance, in other words, of an "invisible hand." Any intervention of the state can only prevent normal adjustments and is therefore a source of waste and misallocation of resources.

The fact that the state will gradually be involved in the maintenance of certain social standards, or even will acquire definite responsibilities to stabilize the economy, does not change the basic fact that growth remains the essential result of the free interaction of market forces.

Even though the federal government has, at times, taken the responsibility of setting up a Crown Corporation in a strategic sector, or of helping the development of certain activities, the main line of reasoning has not really changed. In this regard it is quite remarkable that we have never accepted a practice of selective credit allocation and that only in the last two years have we come around to a discriminatory tax structure to favour specific areas, industries, and products.

Because our so-called economic philosophy is so fundamentally based upon a certain type of market, it can be helpful at this stage to have a sharp look at the real market and see how it is organized.

A market is by definition the meeting of what can be termed economic agents. Concentration has tended over the years to limit considerably the number of agents in the market, or rather, it has given enormous weight to some of them. It is a well-known fact that three or four dozen large corporations are responsible in Canada for a great part of production in industry and resource production. If we add to these large corporations, the federal government, a handful of provinces, and a few large municipalities, we are faced with the real authorities of our economic life. As far as investment decisions are concerned, for instance, they belong to the extent of nearly thirty per cent to the public authorities and for most of the rest to a small band of very large firms

In many ways, we are reluctant to accept this fact. We prefer to think that Combine Investigation Laws will prevent the big from being bad, that financial help to small busines will allow the little fishes to grow bigger. In other words, we just won't face up to a naked and very potent reality: the market where free forces and small firms could adjust to each other is dead. This market of bygone days did not have to be directed by the authorities because its mechanism was automatic; each player was lost in the crowd. Because a small number of players have now an overwhelming influence on the rules of the game, the market has become administered. The problem is to know who is going to administer it and in the interest of whom.

To put the question in such a way implies already an answer. A market led by large firms may or may not operate in the best public interest. The old theories used to say that perfect competition was always in the best public interest. They never even sugested that free enterprise as such had the same result. Granted that free enterprise in a perfect market was the ultimate in economic efficiency; but free enterprise—in the old sense of the word—in a highly concentrated and administered market may or may not be efficient. It requires an umpire, a framework, a set of rules. In other words it requires planning. And planning is not more than that: the establishment of a complete series of specific goals that are compatible with each other, a mix of regulations and incentives, and proper co-ordination so that the goals can be reached even though they may not be compatible with the best interests of the large firms or of several of the public authorities involved.

The necessity of planning can be reached through more specific channels than those already indicated, but channels that originate in the same line of thought. Here, however, we must draw a sharp difference between the private and the public sector.

Private business in Canada has largely become foreign-owned business. This is not to say that there are not thousands of Canadian-owned firms, but in so far as two-thirds of the capital invested in manufacturing, mining, and oil is controlled from abroad, the logical approximation is to emphasize foreign control. It is usually achieved through direct investments and in 1953 a survey established that 60 per cent of all foreign direct investment came from 25 companies. There is no reason to believe that at present the situation may have changed appreciably.

Most of these companies are, of course, American and this raises a very serious problem. I am not referring here to the usual argument of the preservation of a national entity. This is far beyond the scope of the present paper. Rather one must see this phenomenon in the light of economic development and the broad goals of the Canadian economy.

It is perfectly understandable that large U.S. firms should organize— one could even say plan—their operations on a continental basis. Taking into account the tariff nuisance, it is obvious that production, sales, and exports should be so distributed that costs will be as low as possible. This rationality is often, although not necessarily so, incompatible with the logic of Canadian development in so far as we have tried to create, possibly with some illusions, an east-west axis of development over the last century, while, if it were not for the remnants of our custom duties, continental planning by large firms would frequently run in a north-south direction.

Roughly speaking, large foreign corporations are involved in two main fields of activity: manufacturing and resource development. It would be too much to ask from the former that they leave their subsidiaries completely free to determine their markets here and abroad, the rate of technological change, and their production requirements. Subsidiaries cannot always be run that way. And so, it has happened in the past that, for the sake of cost minimization, exports of Canadian subsidiaries have been curtailed, for instance, or the change in techniques slowed down. Of course, one could point to opposite examples where exactly the reverse has occurred: foreign control having helped exports and technological change. The only point I wish to make here is that such decisions have little to do with purely national objectives, may or may not be in the public interest, and we have precious little influence on them anyway.

As far as resource development is concerned, the same conclusion applies in possibly a more dramatic setting. For several of our raw materials the planning by private firms is done on a world-wide basis. The response of Canadian investment in these fields to a change in international demand is in fact the result, in many sectors, of a choice made by a company between alternative possibilities in many countries. Here again we tend to see the booms and busts of natural resource investment as the automatic adjustments to the international markets. In many fields this is not so. Such fluctuations are the result of well-studied decisions between possible sources.

Similarly it would be quite wrong to assume that because Canada is rich in resources, these resources are necessarily less expensive in this country. They often only are if the owner of the resources sells them to subsidiaries or associates. For a Canadian manufacturer they may be as expensive, or in some cases even more expensive, than they would be in the United States or in the United Kingdom.

Pricing policies also are frequently continental in character.

All this leads us to the conclusion that what is good for a Canadian subsidiary can fairly clearly be assumed to be good for the parent company. It may, or may not be good for the U.S. government, and sooner or later we have to ask ourselves whether it is all that good for this country. At least it is not always obvious. Our position until now has been that it was better than nothing, and admittedly it is. But could it be better and—let's face it—are there not cases where it is downright unacceptable?

Obviously the Canadian government and/or provincial governments have had to intervene in many circumstances. Sometimes intervention has taken place in the open, such as the quasi-ultimatum served by the Minister of Commerce to the oil companies with respect to their markets recently. More often it has taken the form of *ad hoc* discussions, reactions to lobbying, and compromises. No systematic approach has been devised, however, and there is still no mechanism by which the plans of large corporations, whether foreign-owned or not, can be fitted into a broad public plan of development.

The actual process through which this goal can be achieved is not likely to be imported from abroad. We shall have to find our own way to negotiate and to induce. But negotiate and induce we will do sooner or later, as the myth of the perfect market gradually vanishes from our nostalgic eyes.

Lest I should be considered as a rabid nationalist, I now want to deal with another field of our economy, and plant banderillas into another bull. So let us turn to the public sector. I stated previously that thirty per cent of all investments in this country originates from it. Yet, here again, we are faced with considerable disorganization after making, over the last fifteen years, efforts to avoid it.

Just after World War II a philosophy became widespread in this country that the federal government was now responsible to the whole of the country for two objectives that were by then prevalent in all of the Western world: social security and economic stabilization. By and large junior governments, although vested with definite constitutional responsibilities, were considered to be marginal economic agents which were, if not officially at least in practice, expected to divest themselves of some of their direct activities for the sake of national efficiency and the attainment of minimum standards of social services throughout the country. Admittedly a considerable backlog of public works had built up during the depression and the war, so that junior governments might be hard put for a while. Eventually, however, things would sort themselves out.

For several years, this thesis of centralized economic power in Ottawa was upheld.

It became rapidly clear, however, that some of the levers which the federal government could use were of limited efficiency. The controls over public works and, generally speaking, public investment did not go very far. On the one hand, provinces and municipalities spent large sums without being unduly sensitive to the objectives of the central government with which in fact they were not closely associated. On the other hand, several Crown corporations acted—and Canadian citizens were proud of this achievement—exactly like private enterprises. Some of them were indeed so refined as to invest in times of prosperity and reduce work during recessions, which is a peculiar way indeed to run a public sector.

Yet a far more omnious development was occurring during the 1950's. What amounts to a major revolution in our affluent society was under way. Canadians generally were less and less satisfied to define the growth of the economy in terms of so many cars per hundred people, or so many radios per household. Acute social needs were being incorporated in our definition of economic development. Our cars required divided highways. Our children felt miserable in any school that was more than ten years old. Cities rebuilt their central areas and developed their suburbs according to the most expensive of all formulas in terms of public works: that of the detached bungalow. All services from urban transit to hospitals had to be expanded, modernized or rebuilt, and all of this had to be done at the same time.

In so far as that was what the citizens wanted, they got it. But an acute problem arose. Nearly all of these social services came under provincial or municipal jurisdiction!

The fiscal system which had emerged from the war was hopelessly inadequate to deal with this enormous financial pressure that was developing among the junior governments. It was thus unavoidable that they should come clamouring to Ottawa for help. They got unconditional payments but they also got money under the so-called joint plans. Within six years the total transfers of the federal government were multiplied 2½ times, and under the system of joint plans expenditures were multiplied by seven. This year for the first time transfers to prov-

61

inces under the form of tax abatements or cash payments are the largest item of the federal budget, well ahead of national defence.

Largely because of this development, the federal government went hopelessly in the red. And provinces as well as municipalities were under such pressures that, in spite of federal help, they had to increase their debt nearly threefold in the last eight years. In fact, if this goes on, the public debt of junior governments will be very shortly as large as that of the federal government itself.

In a centralized state such an explosion of public spending could never have developed in this fashion. Orders of priorities would have been set which might have been irrational in so far as politics are often irrational, but at any rate would have existed. When, for example, the present French government agrees to organize its own nuclear deterrent, it knows that some social or public services will need to be postponed or curtailed to make way for the new project.

Nothing of the kind exists in this country. The federal government sees no reason to curtail its own responsibilities in the face of the outstanding expansion of provincial needs; all governments of this country manage, one way or another, by hook or by crook, to get what they want. And when the financial pressure is too great, the escape hatch of U.S. financing is always available. In fact, foreign borrowing has been found by us to be a powerful tool in order to avoid establishing a proper order of priorities and a clash between the various levels of government. To that extent Confederation as we know it and as we practice it actually finds essential support in the availability of funds in the New York financial markets.

Be it as it may, the sheer economic weight of junior governments has become too great for the federal government to keep up the sort of exclusive responsibilities it had some years ago towards general economic conditions in the country. We have reached a point where the sort of centralization we have known in the past can only spell inefficiency and lack of co-ordination. What is now centralized under a single centre of decision is a small part indeed of the economic weight of public authorities in the economy, certainly less than a fourth of all public investments.

In fact, we might eventually be faced with anti-cyclical federal policies that are only sufficient to counteract the cyclical behaviour of other levels of government. If that ever happened we would have reached the limits of the ludicrous.

We will thus have to establish some new form of co-operation between the various large public authorities particularly in the field of large investment projects. Here again, to avoid useless disorder, we must plan. For obvious political reasons, this is not going to be an easy task. It may require a form of negotiation very much different from what has been known until now in which federal-provincial relations were of a paternalistic nature, the provinces being divided between the nice kids and the awful brats.

In other words, the various spending plans of the public authorities must be made compatible with each other and with the conditions prevailing in the Canadian economy.

It is all the more important that we tend to give increasing attention nowadays to regional disparities in economic growth and in standards of living. This is the third and last aspect of economic organization which I wish to raise here with respect to planning.

In so far as we have had an economic philosophy in the last fifteen years, it has largely been concerned with global policies. Because the federal government was responsible for the whole of the economy it could not and would not discriminate between the regions of Canada in fiscal or in monetary matters, except in very few instances. What we were really concerned with was, as a newspaper reporter once said, the size and not the shape of our cake. Equalization payments were made to the poorer provinces to allow them to bring up their social services to the national level, but the economy generally was viewed as a whole. Large firms distributed their operations across the country as they saw fit.

Behind this attitude lies another implicit assumption. We were convinced that, even though such an approach is likely to produce a very unequal distribution of economic activities in the country, factors of production and particularly labour were mobile enough to drift gradually from depressed areas to those of rapid development. I do not want to suggest here that this assumption was always spelled out in great detail, but it does permeate, to mention only one example, some parts of the Gordon Commission's *Report*.

When the economic development of this country faltered after 1957, regional problems that had often been drowned until then in general prosperity became very acute indeed, and astounding pockets of unemployment started to appear in some areas. Labour, after all, had much less mobility than we thought. In the Maritimes and in Quebec particularly, unemployment became a powerful incentive to local government action.

The idea of regional planning and economic organization started to spread timidly at first and then with growing insistence. Possibly, the

Province of Quebec is the most advanced at the moment in that direction. Not that achievements are already striking, but the authorities and the pubilc have accepted the idea of planning more readily than other parts of the country. There are of course reasons other than economic for this! The wave of nationalism that has developed is not foreign to the spread of the concept of planning itself.

In any case a plan is now being set up. Electricity will be nationalized largely to reorganize the whole structure of rates across the province, a semi-public Investment Corporation has been put into operation, work has started on the project of a steel mill, and studies are being made to assess the possibilities of industrial decentralization.

In so far as this sort of regional emphasis gains in intensity, the problem of co-ordination becomes correspondingly acute, so that planning at the federal level with few references to regional projects and plans might not only create considerable confusion; it might also be largely ineffective.

Thus we cannot escape the conclusion that economic planning in Canada, while undoubtedly necessary, is going to be a very complex operation. The agreement over accepted objectives will be difficult because of the diversity if not the opposition of regional interests. The organization of a framework for business decisions will run against the powerful forces that foreign ownership of our industries has developed. The establishment of new relationships between the various levels of governments so as to associate to a certain extent their economic decisions is a baffling problem for which old formulas are completely inadequate.

If one adds to such difficulties the further obstacles of our perennial constitutional struggles on the one hand, and, on the other, the fact that public opinion and the business world are far from being convinced that planning is an urgent matter, then, it seems to me, we are still a long way from a clear-cut decision on the matter. We may have a national planning board of a kind but it is likely to be more of an illusion for a long time than a reality, as long as we have not acquired the tools necessary to deal with some of the fundamental aspects of the Canadian economy which I have attempted to describe. Planning in any country is difficult, particularly in the opening phases. Planning a foreign-controlled economy is very difficult indeed. But planning a foreign-controlled economy with a federal constitution is a challenge that can be met only after a drastic revolution has taken place in the minds of the people. It may be that the Canadian economy will need to receive severe shocks before we feel forced to get down to it.

H. Ian Macdonald

We have accepted from Europe the lesson that planning need not imply any antithesis between socialism and free enterprise.

During recent months, prominent voices from Canadian business have joined those of labour in urging that "economic planning" is a necessary antidote to many of our economic and social ills. Although such a prescription is certainly not regarded as a panacea, there is a strong implication that, because economic planning appears to have worked so efficiently and successfully elsewhere, it follows that Canada could profit from an injection of the same remedy. At times, it has become difficult to disentangle the ingredients of economic planning from the simpler plea for more co-operation between business, labour, and government. What is clear, however, is that organized planning of economic output and production, which was once regarded as the preserve of socialists, has now become acceptable to all political parties and indeed to most interested groups in the economic community, including the leaders of large business organizations.

It is instructive to consider some of the recent features of our economic life that have stimulated the new wave of interest and, in particular, induced business to espouse planning. In the first place, the existence of chronic unemployment in Canada has reinforced our awareness that private enterprise alone cannot solve all the economic problems of a complex, advanced economy. On the other hand, it is obviously in the best interests not only of society but also of the business community to take measures that will reduce the incidence and impact of this social disease. In turn, Canadians are agreed that government would be greatly strengthened in working towards a solution of this perennial problem if the support of business could be enlisted.

However, political parties must be forthright in their recognition of the fact that economic growth through economic planning will not necessarily solve the problem of unemployment in Canada. The words "growth" and "planning" themselves contain no magic formula that will guarantee success. In 1962, the Canadian economy produced an apparent paradox: the Gross National Product increased by nearly eight per cent, a high rate of economic growth by any yardstick, notwithstanding the persistence of serious pockets of unemployment across the country. In fact, we must recognize the possibility that the curse of unemployment may only be relieved by a deliberate willingness to support economic production where it could not be justified on purely economic grounds. Suppose, for example, that we are considering measures to facilitate the location of industry or to encourage investment in an economic development project, either through the provision of strong incentives or through a public investment board. Now we find that costs of production will be lower in area A, but there is serious unemployment in area B. We are faced with a clear choice of objectives since in Canada it is unrealistic to expect that the unemployed people can be readily transferred.

In that sense, then, full employment must be purchased at the price of less than maximum efficiency. Similarly, a high rate of economic growth may be achieved only through acceptance of some degree of inflation. In another case, stability in the exchange rate may be secured only through a willingness to sustain a higher level of imports than is desirable in terms of the balance of payments. Finally, where so much of Canadian economic activity is dependent on the behaviour of foreign investors in Canada and on the condition of our export markets, we must recognize that there are limits to the influence which planning can have on our economic performance.

In all such cases, economic planning must be based on quite explicit objectives or goals, and the plan must spell out not only the gains but also the costs. Moreover, it must be made abundantly clear that economic planning offers no assurance that all economic goals or social objectives can be attained at once. Choices must still be made and some scale of priorities must always be established. In all cases, the planners as well as the politicians should explain clearly their objectives and their priorities. If we then encounter serious conflicts in our economic and social values, the resolution of those conflicts must remain the prerogative of the people.

The second reason for the present concern about planning might be termed the fallacy of false association. Countries that have recently enjoyed a high rate of economic growth are countries where there has been economic planning. Thus, economic planning receives the credit for high rates of economic growth, particularly in Western Europe. It is assumed that if we plan, we too will have a high rate of economic growth. However, this is gross oversimplification and inadequate generalization. The degree of planning itself has varied substantially in different places. In France, *le plan* exercises considerable direction over the pattern of economic events; in Holland and Sweden on the other hand, emphasis has been concentrated on wages policy. In Western Germany, there is actually no formal planning although remarkable co-operation between government, business, and labour has effectively underwritten the "German economic miracle."

However, "growthmanship" is now a popular economic cult in North America, not only with economists but also with businessmen. The result has been a subtle change in emphasis from the notion that business will produce the best results as long as there is no interference from government to the notion that business will produce the best results provided that there is proper co-operation between business, labour, and government. Unfortunately, we have been unable to define precisely how far that co-operation should go. On the other hand, we have at least accepted from Europe the lesson that planning need not imply any antithesis between socialism and free enterprise. Rather, it means the creation of a climate in which there is a "planned system of free competition" so that co-operation is directed to the greater success of the business community. In this sense, useful planning means that the steel industry can profit greatly from knowing the intentions of the automobile industry and of other sections of the economy.

In the third place, we have now had some modest experience with economic planning in the form of the National Productivity Council. Notwithstanding its good intentions, the council has not had sufficient teeth to affect industrial policy or activity. As a result, many Canadians have drawn the inference that we require some device with greater directive capacity. This suggestion immediately raises the question of the purpose and the extent of the *dirigiste* approach; it also points to the danger that directive planning may be approved for the wrong reasons. For example, we have some evidence to suggest that, within the business community, planning is regarded as a convenient device to reduce some of the impediments which labour and government have placed in its path. To the businessman, then, co-operation implies that some means should be sought to reduce government taxes and prevent wage increases in times of slow economic growth.

There is also an underlying suspicion that the business community might view planning as a convenient way of flouting the Combines Laws. Whether we plan by central commission or by the development council technique, business could well be involved in greater consultation and exchange of information. To that extent, there would be opportunities for close collaboration that might ultimately thwart competition of the sort that would contribute most to economic growth. Therefore, one of the prerequisites of planning should be the preservation of the basic goals of competition, innovations, and incentives to achieve lower costs rather than higher prices. It is quite possible that greater co-operation within Canadian business in the sense of rationalization, where some firms produce only a few products of a special style on a larger scale, would be desirable. However, in that case, we must also permit more foreign competition to assure the consumer of a favourable price level.

There appears to be a tendency in Canada to consider the forms of planning which we might most suitably borrow and adapt to our needs. We must be very cautious not to draw false lessons or raise false hopes through borrowing out of context. Canadian economic problems, if not unique, are at least very special in character. Broadly speaking, success will be determined by adherence to two principles. In the first place, any plan will be acceptable to business firms only if it is drawn up in detail after consultation with business; it must never be treated as something primarily for government. In the second place, it is important that such planning be done by a group that is subordinate to, but outside, the direct sphere of government; for example, it should follow the model of the Bank of Canada rather than the Department of Finance.

In Canada, we face the added problem of co-ordinating dominion-provincial relations in any planning scheme. Since our main problems are largely related to resource development and fiscal policy, we must have as a primary condition genuine co-operation between all levels of government. Nowhere is this more apparent than in our present requirements for municipal development. In his study, *American Capital and Canadian Resources*, Professor Hugh Aitken speaks of "a conflict between provincial and federal concepts of how economic development should come about—a conflict that remains latent as long as federal policy tends to advance the economic interests of the provinces but becomes explicit whenever the federal government, in the interests of preserving national unity, takes action that injures or retards provincial development." We still have a long way to go in resolving these conflicts, and *a fortiori*, in adapting to some acceptable techniques for planning.

Planning is now a respectable word, accepted by business as well as by labour. However, acceptance in principle is not sufficient to solve the problems which confront the Canadian economy at this time. The immediate task is its definition and application. Does planning mean greater co-ordination of investment decisions by Canadian corporations? Does it imply rationalization of production, thereby providing for greater specialization and division of labour? Does it require a "national wages policy" which would be endorsed by business as well as by labour? We have so far been starved for the practical suggestions, without which planning must remain a hollow concept in Canada.

Carl A. Pollock

Let us at all cost steer clear of the kind of regimentation
associated with the centrally directed and planned economy.

As spokesman for a national organization [The Canadian Manufacturers' Association] which subscribes to a private enterprise way of life, I want first to be completely clear in my own mind as to what is meant by the question "Does Canada Need Planning?" If the suggestion is that this country's future must of necessity be intertwined with a planned economy, which is just another way of describing socialistic regimentation, then my answer is an unequivocal no and I might as well stop right now. On the other hand if an affirmative answer to the question visualizes the establishment of realistic economic assessments and careful fiscal planning which would result in the optimum use of all our resources both natural and human, then I say by all means let's examine the need.

All of us, whether in our private lives as consumers or in our public lives as producers, are constantly planning and a lot of it comes under the heading of economic planning. At the national level a case can certainly be made for the type of indicative consultative planning which will provide better incentives for the encouragement of new production, new plants, more exports, and more jobs. And so it is that in this country we have been taking a hard look at how they do things in Western Europe. And well and good we might do so. I am all for learning from people's operations, profiting from their experiences, doing our own thinking, and then adapting those parts, if any, which lend themselves to Canadian requirements.

However, without disparaging what has been achieved in Western Europe, there are two widely held assumptions which I would question. One is that European type planning policies are necessarily transferable *in toto* to Canada. And the other is that these policies have solved all the economic problems of the countries which have followed them. As to the first I would say this. There are vital built-in differences between the Canadian economy and the economies of industrial Western Europe, and indiscriminate importation of planning policies without due consideration of Canadian requirements would be unthinkable. To give but one important example, each of our European competitors is a highly industrialized, compact, and relatively small country; whereas Canada has to produce for a thinly populated domestic market scattered over four thousand miles and in every respect influenced and conditioned to an enormous degree by a neighbour which just happens to be the largest and wealthiest industrial nation on the face of the earth. As to the second assumption, while Western Europe as a whole has certainly not had the serious unemployment which we have had, it is not true that it is economically trouble-free. Take Britain, France, Western Germany, Belgium, Holland, and Sweden: there is not one of these countries of which it can be said that it is not concerned either about productivity or inflation, production costs or strikes, or that very important matter, the rate of economic growth. And while I am fully aware of our own economic problems, it is of some significance that not one of these countries which I have mentioned matched Canada's nearly 7 per cent real increase in economic growth in 1962.

Let's always keep the relevant facts very much in focus. And so to the question "Does Canada Need Planning?" I would return this answer: it all depends on what you mean by planning.

Private and corporate planning last year resulted in the investment in Canada of five thousand million dollars. This is the kind of planning which makes our economy tick and which has given us in the North American continent the highest standard of living on record in the world. We need as much of it as we can get. But one of the main attributes of our system is the freedom it gives us to be flexible and adaptable, and so if we refine (and we can refine) and improve this kind of private enterprise planning, the success of which depends on the co-operation of labour, management, and government, and if the policies of these three segments of our society are co-ordinated in such a way as to promote stable and adequate growth without damage to the free market mechanism (which after all is the basis of our system), then by all means let us do so. The measure of establishing in Canada the national economic development council, a consultative and co-ordinating body, could well be the answer to the question. But let us at all cost steer clear of the kind of regimentation associated with the centrally directed and planned economy.

Clarence L. Barber

Effective economic planning is more likely to be handi-capped in the future by deeply ingrained prejudices about what governments should or should not do than by our in-ability to determine what correct economic policy should be.

Viewed from the perspective of the last twenty years, it is clear that for effective government economic planning in Canada three things are essential. We need sound and imaginative economic advice, public understanding and acceptance of the recommended policies, and a government prepared to make decisions and implement the required policies after seasoning and modifying them with appropriate garnishes of political considerations. Let us review briefly the federal government's record in this field since 1939 and try to determine what has gone wrong. For it is now clear to almost every Canadian that something has gone wrong.

During the war and in some degree in the early post-war period all of the above three requirements were fulfilled. Faced with a wartime emergency the government sought and obtained expert economic advice. Many economists left the universities to serve in Ottawa during this period, and there they were joined by able business executives and other experts. Although many of the measures adopted were unpopular, the government was able through the press and radio to convince people they were needed. And once the period of the phoney war ended the government acted quickly and effectively to implement required policies. The result was a war effort that compares favourably with that of any other country.

But as the post-war period proceeded something began to go wrong. In the main, I think the difficulty has been with the public discussion and understanding of the economic issues and with the choice of an appropriate blend of political and economic elements rather than with the quality of the economic advice itself, although even this may have become conservative and unimaginative. One cannot be sure about the quality of the advice, of course, because it is given in secret and even the economic studies on which it is based are rarely available to people outside the government service. (For this reason I would fully endorse a recent recommendation for the Glassco Commission that more of these government research studies be published as they are in the United States.) One is conscious too that many of the able young economists who joined the civil service early in the war are still there and now occupy positions of the first importance. But it may be that unlike distilled spirits economists do not improve with age. The constant grinding effects of administrative routines and political horse-trading must make it extremely difficult to retain a live contact with the latest results of economic theorists and research workers around the world.

Evidence that something had gone wrong can be found in some of the bases on which Prime Minister Diefenbaker fashioned his victory in 1957. I am thinking here of his attack on the bureaucrats who were running the country, his criticism of government surpluses as over-taxation, and his gleeful taunt of the six-buck boys, a reference to the $6 increase in old age pensions that the Liberal administration enacted just before the election. There may, of course, have been some sub-stance to at least two of these charges. It is said that Finance Minister Harris genuinely believed that the country could not afford an increase in pensions of more than $6. If he was advised to this effect by govern-ment economists he was clearly ill-advised. And although senior govern-ment economists were not running the country, it may have been true that a government long in power had come to rely too much on eco-nomic advice, giving insufficient attention to political considerations. But this was not the fault of the economic advisers. The alleged over-taxation had no basis at all, although it may well have been a politically popular charge. For with a decline in government saving (the shift from surpluses to deficits), Canada has come to depend increasing on foreign savings to finance her capital investment (which hardly squares with a "Made in Canada" label).

The weakness of Canadian economic planning is underlined by the events that lead up to the exchange crisis in June 1962. In retrospect it is clear that over the past four or five years [1958–9 to and including 1962] a major goal of the federal government should have been to reduce Canada's balance of payments deficit and our dependence on foreign capital. If such a policy had been implemented from 1958 on, Canada would have had a much lower level of unemployment, a more satisfactory rate of growth and much smaller government deficits. With such a policy the exchange emergency would never have occurred.

Almost everyone now recognizes the truth of this argument. Why then were the government and economists in general so slow to recog-nize that this was the appropriate policy? It ought to have been clear at once. And yet all the evidence points to the fact that almost everyone in Canada failed to see the situation in its proper perspective. I have recently canvassed a number of periodicals over the period 1958 to 1961 and nowhere have I been able to find before 1961 a clear and forthright analysis of the problem. In the *Canadian Forum*, for example, there are numerous short articles on the current economic situation by able young economists at the University of Toronto but not one gives a clear analysis of the relation between monetary policy, the exchange rate, and Canada's unemployment problem. Few of them recognize the relationship at all.

Or, to take another example, when the Senate Committee held its hearings on Canada's unemployment problem in the fall of 1960 no one presented to the committee a clear and explicit analysis of the bearing of our balance of payments deficit on the unemployment problem or underlined the need for a depreciation in the exchange rate. Some of the presentations mentioned a lower value of the dollar in passing, but not in a manner which indicated they understood the problem. And indeed, one can find a number of instances of prominent economists who argued that the forces leading to a balance of payments deficit were not the source of our difficulties.

Given this failure in economic intelligence on the part of our professional economists, it is not surprising that the discussion of the issues in the press and in popular periodicals was completely inadequate. For there is not a single newspaper in Canada whose opinion is worth taking seriously on economic questions of any depth or subtlety. This is a deplorable situation and a serious handicap for a country that would like to have effective economic planning. But there it is. Nor are matters helped by the gobs of free but ill-informed economic advice handed out by our Chambers of Commerce, our Manufacturers' Association, and by presidents of some of our large corporations. As long as these organizations are not prepared to base their statements on competent professional economic advice they should keep quiet. Their behaviour at the moment in this area is merely irresponsible.

If you think these remarks are extreme, let me say that I firmly believe that effective economic planning is more likely to be handicapped in the future by deeply ingrained prejudices about what governments should or should not do than by our inability to determine what correct economic policy should be. We laugh at superstitious and primitive natives who hold rain dances and conduct fertility rites, but many of these native superstitions are no more unscientific than the views of many Canadians about the dangers of government deficits.

What then can we do to create conditions in Canada more favourable to effective economic planning? I would like to recommend three measures. First, we need a large increase in the funds available to support economic research in Canadian universities. Economists on the staff of Canadian universities are now so overburdened with teaching and thesis supervision that they have little or no time for independent research and writing. There is not a single economic research Chair in a Canadian University. And the funds available to support economic research are infinitesimal compared with the money that is provided to support research in the natural sciences. Second, we need an economic planning board which would be staffed almost entirely by professional economists and which would be free to publish periodic reports on the state of the Canadian economy and on economic problems of special interest to Canada. Finally, we need a substantial improvement in the quality of economic discussion in the press, in our periodicals, and on television and radio. I would hope that the publication of readable reports by the economic planning board would help to raise the level of public discussion. But it would be a help, too, if newspapers would occasionally hire competent economists to write their economic commentary. And how business organizations such as the Canadian Manufacturers' Association think they can get along without professional economists on their staff is more than I can understand. The failure of these organizations to present their economic case effectively in Ottawa has cost them hundreds of millions of dollars in the last few years. And they seem content to let this continue.

Larry Sefton

No nation can fill the needs of its people and meet its commitments to the world in the twentieth century unless it develops democratic economic planning as a nation.

In the last three or four years the word "planning" has become a stock word in our vocabulary. Earlier the idea of a planned economy, and therefore the word "planning" itself, was frowned upon and anyone advocating economic planning was considered, if not a dangerous radical, at least a nut. The proposition that a degree of planning is necessary by the different interests in our society to solve some of our major problems such as unemployment has now caught on. The question now being disputed is: how much planning?

Businessmen have done some planning to meet the market potential for their product. In some larger undertakings such as the steel industry and others, management has attempted to plan in longer terms than a year to expand plant capacity in an orderly way so that it can keep up to new and expanded product demands.

Labour for years has been promoting the idea of planning for our social needs on a national and provincial basis. We in the labour movement have urged the introduction of Medicare plans, to refer to a current issue, with all Canadians contributing and receiving medical services as they need them and not whether they can afford them. Social measures, such as hospital care, unemployment insurance, workmen's compensation, mothers' allowance, and others, have been promoted by labour because they highlight the planned use of the resources available to provide benefits to all members of our society.

In the last few years we have had continuing unemployment, and, although it has eased up somewhat in the summers, it has remained at a level that is completely unjustified for a country that prides itself on its high standard of living. The labour movement, through action at its conventions has repeatedly warned governments and the public that the introduction of new technology and the continued automation of our industry on an unplanned basis would cause unemployment. I believe it is because of the unemployment that just "won't disappear" and because of increased competition from abroad that the idea of some planning in our economy has taken hold.

Last summer, a management-labour-government mission to Europe, in which I took part, found that the very countries we fear competitively accept planning in varying degrees as basic to their economic needs. In these countries there is a close bond between industry and labour and a high degree of co-operation between the two of them and the government. Labour is accepted on equal terms with management as an economic partner. There is full employment. Benefits of increasing productivity accrue to all sectors of the economy. This degree of co-operation does not exist in Canada; labour is not accepted as an equal partner. The current productivity drive is one-sided, for labour is not even adequately represented on the National Productivity Council. Workers are offered no reward for greater efforts in the plants, mines, and mills.

I believe most emphatically that we must resort to democratic economic planning to overcome the country's major problems, one being current unemployment and the other being the creation of new jobs for our expanding work force. We unionists do not dread the automation of our industry. We believe man should be master of his destiny and the machine made the slave of man rather than the reverse. But if automation is permanently to enlarge our jobless rolls it will serve no social good. We in the labour movement have been trying to cope on a plant-by-plant basis with the dislocation caused by technological advances. It cannot be done this way. Employers strenuously resist accepting responsibility for retraining people who are displaced to fit them for jobs on new equipment. And even if they accepted this responsibility fully, it would not solve the problems of the employee who is let go permanently.

Employers have also opposed vesting the pension rights of their employees, so that if they are displaced they will not lose out this way too. Supplementary unemployment benefit schemes have been rebuffed by employers, so that men thrown out of work have a greatly reduced income that does not even provide the necessities, let alone any money for consumption of the vast array of goods turned out today. Severance allowances are being denied and, although paid by some companies, they are small and do not provide enough money to tide a man over for a long enough period to get re-located. Employers say: "Why should we pay the fringes when others don't?" Or: "Our job is to run this plant at a profit. We can't be responsible for the rise in general unemployment."

This may all be true. But it is precisely this thinking which surely points up the fact that the interest of everyone—the national interest—demands the kind of planning in our economy that will bring peak efficiency to our industry and full employment to our workers. There is a large market of unfilled needs in Canada that can only be met by a fully employed and well-paid force. The markets of the unfilled needs of the world that now lie at our doorstep are so great that they stagger the imagination.

I submit that no business could exist for very long if the management did not plan its course. I also submit that no nation can fill the needs of its people and meet its commitments to the world in the twentieth century unless it develops democratic economic planning as a nation.

Eric A. Trigg

*Whether we like it or not our planning must recognize the
interests of others, particularly the investors abroad who
own so much of our industry. . . .*

Two countries cited by proponents of planning as outstanding examples
of success are Sweden and France. If we examine some of the reasons
for the degree of their success, we may gain some insight into the problems of planning in Canada.

I believe it would not be disputed that: they both have strong national
identities; they both were aware of, and concerned about, the urgency of
economic and political problems which prevailed in Europe in the
immediate post-war period; they both have deep-rooted histories which
provided a continuing strong desire to control their own destiny as a
nation; there existed in both countries after the war an acceptance on
the part of business, government, and labour (the last with some reluc-
tance of a political nature in France) that they would all benefit by
working together; there was a willingness on the part of government to
institute fiscal, monetary, and tariff policies which would aid industry to
reach agreed targets; and there was a willingness on the part of industry
to accept centralized controls, particularly in the field of finance, which
inevitably meant controls on final investment decisions.

One could state these points in different ways and suggest that our
European friends have long tended towards a socialistic approach and
that the aftermath of World War II left them with few alternatives,
other than the ones they chose. However, having had some experience
with free enterprisers in both countries, I prefer to regard the points
more as a reflection of the basic homogeneous nature of the two countries and, contrasting their structure with that of Canada, it seems to me
that many of our problems with regard to successful planning become
self-evident.

Can we honestly state that Canada and Canadians have a strong sense
of national identity today? Quite apart from the Province of Quebec,
where there is clearly less than full acceptance that Confederation has
worked to the benefit of all Canadians, does the secondary manufacturer of Ontario really have strong common feelings with the prairie

farmer or the people of the Maritimes? Are there signs that the provinces are trying to work ever more closely together on economic matters? Who among us can stand up and say "I am a typical Canadian!"—with emphasis on the adjective?

While Canadians can be proud of their contribution to Allied success in the last war, no Canadian would dispute the fact that many material advantages accrued to the country through the rapid acceleration of industrial development which the war effort required. The post-war investment boom brought ever-improving standards of living and there was little obvious need for consolidating the nation, and little sense of urgency. The years since 1956 have brought more soul-searching as unemployment rose and government deficits began to cumulate, and it is to be hoped that out of our present political chaos a reconciliation of the diverse regional views and interests can be effected.

Apart from the traditional problem of ethnic divergencies, we have the more tangible and obvious problem that, while agricultural and raw material exporters have been worried for years because of over-capacity in Canada, their basic belief that lower tariffs are needed throughout the world is certainly not shared by the protectionist elements in the community who argue that we must build up our secondary industry. Both views can be supported by persuasive arguments, but the shattered political scene, not only in the federal field, but in the long unsettled relationships between the provinces and Ottawa, provides little hope of an early opportunity to reconcile these all-important differences.

To discuss the question of controlling our own destiny is to enter an area of profound emotionalism. Many Canadians have accepted the benefits accruing to us over the years from increased investment and development without examining in any detail whether they, or others, were responsible for this development. Few Canadians, outside the field of economics, would recognize their country if it was described as an under-developed area, but it takes little perusal of international payments statistics to recognize that this country has been, continues to be, and will be heavily dependent upon external finance for many years to come. Canadians may be said to have three basic economic choices:

1. They can withdraw within their own borders, controlling the inflow of foreign capital (and, as a corollary, reducing it) thus accepting a slow rate of progress and perhaps, inevitably, losing an increasing proportion of their better brains to other countries.

2. They can recognize that their best hopes for further development lie in continuing and increasing flows of funds from outside the country,

and search for additional advantages from this policy in the form of increasing access to external markets.

3. Or they can seek a slower, more balanced development and encourage the resumption of large-scale immigration to build a larger domestic market.

Few Canadians would accept the first alternative and, certainly in those parts of the country where there is even now a feeling of being left behind, if this became a national philosophy, a greater impetus would be given to the search for "separatist" alternatives. The third alternative, if acceptable to some, would be difficult to sell to many because it could easily accentuate unemployment problems in some areas in the short term. If accepted as a policy it would have no assurance of success because Canada has lost some of its magic as a place of new residence, not only because of the unemployment experience, but because of improved economic conditions elsewhere.

The implication of the second alternative will generate resistance on emotional grounds, but geography and history have been pushing Canada in this direction and it would be wise for Canadians to consider how they can move with these inexorable forces to advantage, rather than pushing upstream to no long-term avail. Prior to World War II, Canada relied heavily on the triangular trade between Canada, the United Kingdom, and the United States. Despite ever-present goodwill on the part of all participants, the industrial development of Canada and the geographical proximity of the United States have deprived the United Kingdom of a large amount of the growth in Canada's external purchases. The nature of Canadian development is such that the manufactured products of the United Kingdom are bound to suffer. This fact is well recognized in the United Kingdom as applying to many Commonwealth countries, and has had an important part in the decision to seek common ground with the rest of Europe.

At the same time, the need for investment capital has placed an increasing amount of Canadian industry in the hands of American owners—a state of affairs not unusual for any under-developed country. To complain excessively about losing control of our own economic resources in the face of obvious need for additional investment is simply attempting to cut off our noses to spite our faces. We would be much further ahead if we could convince our friends in the United States of the wisdom of providing us with greater access to their markets. Put very simply, we let their capital in here, so it is in their interests to let our products in there. From what evidence I have available, I am not convinced that we are suffering from widespread inefficiency in our secondary industries, but nobody can dispute the fact that a manufacturer in Canada, with his outlets spread across five thousand miles, has more geographic problems to contend with than his counterpart established less than one hundred miles south of the border. Given greater access, surely our own manufacturers could compete.

Rather than working against investments from the United States, cannot we emphasize the advantage to those investors of helping Canada grow from within, as well as from without?

To obtain general acceptance of this alternative, or of a better one, if it can be found, we still have to balance the varied interests of the regional groupings in this country. In other countries, government, business, and labour have worked together towards targets, and it has been a recognized principle that the men from industry who must work towards completion of any plan should have an opportunity to help in setting the targets for the plan. It has also been recognized that governments would conduct their affairs to assist their own industry to achieve the objectives of the plan, not only by fiscal incentives, but by close control of the capital market. It is questionable whether we are large enough and sufficiently strong to do the second, even if we wanted to—and I hope we would not—without physical controls which would bring their own problems. We had an excellent illustration of how little control we had in the exchange crisis of 1962, and there are experienced international authorities on monetary matters who doubt the ability of any nation completely to control its own affairs.

Canada plans now every time a governmental, business, or labour decision is taken. Some co-ordinated planning is needed if only to recognize and discuss the diverse views. But discussion can easily involve the wrong people. As long as provincial and federal authorities are at loggerheads, it is absurd for others to think they can formulate useful plans. Perhaps a start could be made by having provincial authorities each prepare a plan for Canada as a whole, and then trying to bring the individual ideas together. Provincial plans for the provinces alone, outside the federal context, will probably only create more problems.

Whether we like it or not, however, our planning must recognize the interests of others, particularly the investors abroad who own so much of our industry, and the other under-developed countries which rely even more than we on agricultural and raw material exports for their well-being.

These two groups will have plans of their own, and in this world of plan and counterplan, their actions could upset even the best-laid plans of Canadians.

Selected Bibliography

Books

Anshen, M., and F. Wormuth, *Private Enterprise and Public Policy* (United States), New York and Toronto, Macmillan, 1954.

Bauchet, P., *La Planification française, quinze ans d'expérience*, Paris, Editions du Seuil, 1962.

————— *Propriété publique et planification*, Paris, Editions Cujas.

Brewis, T. N., *et al, Canadian Economic Policy*, New York, St. Martin's Press, (Toronto, Macmillan), 1961.

Central Planning Bureau, *Scope and methods of the Central Planning Bureau*, The Hague, 1956.

Cazes, B., *La planification en France et le 4ème Plan*, Paris, Les Editions l'Epargne, 1962.

Conference on Research in Income and Wealth, *Input-Output Analysis: An Appraisal, Studies in Income and Wealth*, vol. 18, Princeton, Princeton University Press for the National Bureau of Economic Research.

Corry, J. A., *The Growth of Government Activities since Confederation: A Study Prepared for the Royal Commission on Dominion Provincial Relations*, Ottawa, King's Printer, 1939.

Dobbs, M. H., *An Essay on Economic Growth and Planning*, London, Routledge & Kegan Paul, 1960.

Economic Planning Agency (Japan), *The New Long Range Economic Plan of Japan*, Tokyo, Japan Times Limited, 1961.

Erhard, L., *Prosperity Through Competition*, 3rd ed., London, Thames & Hudson; (Toronto, British Book Service), 1960.

Fox, S., *The Era of Continuous Prosperity: Economic Control in the Free Enterprise Society*, New York, William-Frederick Press, 1961.

Franks, Sir O. S., *Central Planning in War and Peace*, Cambridge, Harvard University Press, 1947.

Hamlin, D. L. B. (ed.), *The New Europe*, Toronto, University of Toronto Press, 1962.

Hayek, F. A. von, *The Road to Serfdom*, Chicago, University of Chicago Press, 1944.

Jouvenel, B. de, *Planning in France: Techniques and Lessons*, Moorgate and Wall Street, 1961.

Lerner, A. P., *The Economics of Control: Principles of Welfare Economics*, New York, Macmillan, 1944.

Myrdal, G., *Beyond the Welfare State*, New Haven, Yale University Press, (Montreal, McGill University Press), 1960.

Plan for Development, Employment, and Finance in Italy for the Decade 1955–64, Rome, 1955.

Perry, J. H., *Taxes, Tariffs, and Subsidies: A History of Canadian Fiscal Development*, 2 vols., Toronto, University of Toronto Press, 1955.

Political Economic Planning, *European Organizations*, London, Allen and Unwin, (Toronto, Thomas Nelson), 1959.

———— *Regional Development in the European Economic Community*, London, Allen and Unwin (Toronto, Thomas Nelson), 1962.

Royal Commission on Canada's Economic Prospects, Ottawa, Queen's Printer, 1957.

Sennholz, M. H., *On Freedom and Free Enterprise: Essays in Honour of Ludwig von Mises*, Princeton, N.J., Van Nostrand, 1956.

*Shenfield, A. A., *et al.*, *Agenda for Free Society*, London, Hutchinson, 1961.

Social Planning for Canada, Research Committee, League for Social Reconstruction, Toronto, Thomas Nelson, 1935.

Thomson, D., *Democracy in France*, 3rd ed., London, Toronto, Oxford University Press, 1958.

*Tobin, J., *et al.*, *The American Business Creed*, Cambridge, Harvard University Press, 1956.

Wallich, H. C., *The Cost of Freedom: A New Look at Capitalism*, New York, Harper, 1960.

Wootton, B., *Freedom Under Planning*, Chapel Hill, University of North Carolina Press, 1945.

Pamphlets

Commissariat général du plan d'équipement de la productivité, Paris, *Quatrième Plan 1962–63*, la documentation française illustrée, Oct.-Nov. 1962.

Direction de la Documentation, *La Planification française*, Paris (notes et études documentaires), Dec. 1961.

McKinnon, N. J., *Planning and Performance*, Address delivered to the Investment Dealers' Association of Canada, June 18, 1962.

National Productivity Council, *The Report of the Labour-Management-Government Mission to Europe*, Ottawa, 1962.

Perspectives Socialistes, *Planification, socialisme, et démocratie*, Paris, Jan. 1961.

Planning, Papers read at the Business Economists' Conference, Oxford (Robert Shone, P. de Wolff, Pierre Massé, F. W. Paish, T. Wilson), London, Eyre & Spottiswoode, 1962.

Political and Economic Planning, *Economic Planning in France*, London, 1961.

Weldon, J. C., *What is Planning?*, Toronto, The Ontario Woodsworth Memorial Foundation, 1962.

Weldon, J. C., G. W. Cadbury and M. K. Oliver, *Democratic Planning: A Symposium*, Toronto, The Ontario Woodsworth Memorial Foundation, 1962.

Chapters in Books

Brady, A., "The State and Economic Life," in *Canada*, ed. G. W. Brown (The United Nations series, R. J. Kerner, General Editor), Berkeley and Los Angeles, University of California Press, 1950 (353–71).

————"The Constitution and Economic Policy," in *The Canadian Economy and its Problems*, ed. H. A. Innis and A. F. W. Plumtre, Kingston, Jackson Press, 1934 (second printing) (170–81).

Caves, R. E., and R. H. Holton, "Government and Canadian Economic Development," in *The Canadian Economy*, Cambridge, Harvard University Press, 1959 (233–56).

Easterbrook, W. T., and H. G. Aitken, "The Strategy of Canadian Development," in *Canadian Economic History*, Toronto, Macmillan, 1961 (350–408).

*Gordon, H. S., "Planning for Economic Progress," in *Social Purpose for Canada*, ed. M. Oliver, Toronto, University of Toronto Press, 1961 (249–82).

*Conference participant.

Innis, H. A., "Government Ownership and the Canadian Scene," in *Essays in Canadian Economic History*, Toronto, University of Toronto Press, 1956 (78–96).

*Johnson, H. G., "Planning and the Market in Economic Development," in *Money, Trade and Economic Growth*, London, Allen & Unwin, 1962 (151–64). Reprinted from the *Pakistan Economic Journal* 8 (2): 44–55 (June 1958).

Keynes, J. M., "The Social Philosophy Towards Which the General Theory Might Lead," in *The General Theory* . . . , London, Macmillan, 1936 (372–84).

Lamontagne, M., "The Role of Government," in *Canada's Tomorrow*, ed. G. P. Gilmour, Toronto, Macmillan, 1954 (117–52).

Samuelson, P. A., "The Economic Role of Government," in *"Economics: An Introductory Analysis*, 4th ed., New York, Toronto, McGraw-Hill, 1958 (111–40).

Periodical Articles (I)

Abbreviations:

Act Ec   *L'Actualité Economique*, Montreal
AER   *American Economic Review*
BNL   *Banca Nazionale del Lavoro*, Review, Rome
CJEPS   *Canadian Journal of Economics and Political Science*
SEJ   *Southern Economic Journal*, North Carolina
SR   *Social Research*, New York
TAHA   *Annals*, Hitotsubashi Academy, Tokyo
WA   *Weltwirtschaftliches Archiv*, Hamburg

Balogh, T., "Germany, an Experiment in Planning by the *free* price mechanism," *BNL* 3:71–102 (Apr.–June 1950).

*Barber, C. L., "Canada's Post-War Monetary Policy, 1945–54, *CJEPS* 23:349–62 (Aug. 1957).

————— "Canadian Tariff Policy," *CJEPS* 21:513–30 (Nov. 1955).

Beer, S. H., "British Planning under the Labour Government," *SR* 17:35–64 (Mar. 1950).

Bernt, H. H., "Freedom and Planning," *Economic Papers*, Patna University, India, 3(1):28–37 (Apr. 1958).

Carter, C. F., "The Uses of Nick and Neddy," *District Bank Review*, England (Sept. 1962).

Cazes, B., "Capitalisme et planification sont-ils compatibles?," *L'Institut de Science Economique Appliquée*, France (Recherches et dialogues philosophiques et économique, no. 4).

Clauch, S. P., "Economic Planning in a Capitalistic Society from Monnet to Hirsch," *Political Science Quarterly* 4:439–552 (1956).

Clay, Sir H., "Planning and the Market Economy: Recent British experience," *AER/S* 40: 1–22 (May 1950).

Club, J. M., "Rapport sur la nature et le rôle du plan dans une démocratie," Paris, *Revue Les Cahier de la République* (Dec. 1961–Jan.–Feb. 1962).

Condliffe, J. B., "New Zealand's Experiment in Economic Planning," *AER* 47:930–45 (Dec. 1957).

Devons, E., "Planning by Economic Survey," *Economica*, new series, 19:237–52 (Aug. 1952).

Easterbrook, W. T., "Long Period Comparative Study: Some Historical Cases," *Journal of Economic History*, New York, 17(4): 171–95 (Dec. 1957).

Eastman, H. C., "Recent Canadian Economic Policy: Some Alternatives," *CJEPS* 18:135–45 (May 1955).

Eckstein, A., "Individualism and the Role of the State in Economic Growth," *Economic Development and Cultural Change*, Chicago, 6:81–7 (Jan. 1958).

Elliot, J. E., "Economic Planning Reconsidered," *Quarterly Journal of Economics*, Cambridge, Mass., 72: 55–76 (Feb. 1958).

Fowke, U. C., "The National Policy: Old and New," *CJEPS* 18: 271–86 (Aug. 1952).

Galbraith, J. K., "Causes of Economic Growth: The Canadian Case," *Queen's Quarterly*, Kingston, Ont., 65:169–82 (Summer 1958).

Gathercole, G. E., "The Record and Role of Planning in Economic Development," *Canadian Public Administration* (June 1962).

Hayes, H. G., "The Economy, Liberty and the State," *SEJ* 26:147-9 (Oct. 1959).

Heimann, E., "On Economic Planning," *SR* 17:269–92 (Sept. 1950).

————— "The Interplay of Capitalism and Socialism in the American Economy," *SR* 24:87–111 (Apr. 1957).

Kapp, K. W., "Economic Planning and Freedom," *WA* 64:29–52 (1950).

Kierans, E. W., "Wanted: A New Commercial Policy," *Canadian Chartered Accountant* (Apr. 1962).

La Garrigue, V. R., "Les Besoins dans une économie planifiée," *Act Ec* 24:422–38 (Oct. 1948).

Lindall, E., "Swedish Experience in Economic Planning," *AER/S* 40:11–20 (May 1950).

Maier, K. F., "Has Western Germany a Liberal Market Economy?" *BNL* 5:37–43 (Jan.–Mar. 1952).

Mitchell, J., "Economic Planning and the Long-Term Programme," *Review of Economic Studies* 23(1):46–55 (1955).

Musolf, L. D., "Canadian Public Enterprise: A Character Study," *American Political Science Review* 50:405–21 (June 1956).

Myrdal, G., "The Trend Towards Economic Planning," *The Manchester School of Economics and Political Studies* 19:1–42 (1951).

*Parizeau, J., "L'Orientation nouvelle de la politique économique," *Act Ec* 36:522–33 (Oct.–Dec. 1960).

Peacock, A. T., "The Public Sector and the Theory of Economic Growth," *Scottish Journal of Political Economy* 6:1–12 (Feb. 1959).

Pedersen, J., "On the Effects of National Economic Planning on the International Division of Labour," *Economia Internazionale*, Genova, 3:142–55 (Feb. 1950).

Rolfe, S. E., "The Trade Unions, Freedom, and Economic Planning," *Industrial Relations Research Association, Proceedings*, Madison, Wis., 3:338–51 (Dec. 1950).

*Shenfield, A. A., "Nationalization," *Federation of British Industries* (1956).

Schweinitz, K. de, Jr., "Free Enterprise and Democracy," *SR* 20:55–74 (Apr. 1953).

Schweitzer, A., "Theories of Controlled Capitalism," *Kyklos: Internationale Zeitschrift für Sozialwissenschaften*, Basel, 9:492–505 (1956).

Scott, F. R., "Constitutional Adaptations to Changing Functions of Government," *CJEPS* 11:329–41 (Aug. 1945).

Sethur, F., "Trade Unionism and Central Planning in Western Europe: Practical Socialism and Planning," *SEJ* 22:221–9 (Oct. 1955).

Sohmen, E., "Competition and Growth: The Lesson of West Germany," *AER* 49:986–1003 (Dec. 1959).

Surányi-Unger, T., "Measuring Economic Freedom and Planning," *WA* 66:245–90 (1951).

Svennilson, I., *et al.*, "Long-Term Planning in Sweden," *Skandinaviska Banken* 43(3) (1962).

Taylor, R. W., "Central Economic Co-ordination in British Government," *SR* 21:179–203 (July 1954).

*Tobin, J., "National Goals and Economic Policy," *Papers Presented at Second National Farm Policy Review Conference*, North Carolina State College, 2–38 (Nov. 1961).

Urquhart, M. C., "Public Investment in Canada," *CJEPS* 11:535–53 (Nov. 1945).

Wellisz, S., "Economic Planning in the Netherlands, France, and Italy," *Journal of Political Economy*, Chicago (June 1960).

Yamada, Y., "On the Five-Year Economic Plan in Japan: Some Methodological Considerations," *TAHA* 7:33–45 (Oct. 1950).

————— "On the Method of the Economic Plan (1958–62) of Japan," *TAHA* 10:21–56 (Aug. 1959).

Periodical Articles (II)

Arès, R., "Pour une planification humaine de l'économie," *Relations* (Nov. 1961).

Berkinshaw, R. C., "Plans, Not Miracles Build Canada's Future," digest of an address, *Financial Post* 48:22 (Nov. 6, 1954).

"C.L.C. Urges Public Plan for Economic Growth," *Canadian Labour* 7:27 (Nov. 1962).

Cardien, J. R., "Possibilités et conditions de collaboration entre les agents de l'économie," *Relations Industrielles* (Oct. 1960).

"Du Rôle économique de l'état Québecois," editorial, *Relations* 228:311–12 (Dec. 1959).

Drummond, I. M., "Can Labour-Management Co-operation Solve Our Economic Problems?," *Canadian Forum* (Jan. 1963).

"Europe Charts Its Business Future," *Business Week* (April 7, 1962).

Fenton, A., "Economic Planning in Free Societies," *Canadian Business* (Feb. 1963).

Jodoin, C., "Labour and Management Must Work Together," *Canadian Forum* (Feb. 1960).

Little, A. J., "What Government Can Do To Aid the Nation's Growth," *Canadian Business* (Nov. 1961).

*Macdonald, H. I., "Planning: The Challenge to Business," *Saturday Night* (June 23, 1962).

Parenteau, R., "L'Expérience européene de planification, peut-elle nous servir?," *Cité Libre* (Oct. 1962).

Pépin, J. L., "La planification decentralisée, nouveau paradoxe canadien," *Le Magazine Maclean* 1:4 (Oct. 1961).

"Planned Europe," *Economist* (May 5, 1962).

"Planning, by Whom?," *Economist* (Aug. 26, 1961).

Raskin, A. H., "Our Economy: Mixed and Mixed-up," *Reporter* (Oct. 11, 1962).

Reid, M., "Why We Need a Flexible Economic Plan," *Financial Post* 49:15 (Feb. 12, 1955).

Steinthorsen, D. H., "Problems in Input-Output Analysis of the Canadian Economy," unpublished Ph.D. dissertation, Harvard University, 1954.

Taylor, E. P., "Is an Economics Ministry Our Biggest Need Now?," digest of an address, *Financial Post* (Oct. 7, 1962).

*Tobin, J., "Growth through Taxation," *New Republic* (July 1960).

"When Business and Government Team Up," *U.S. News and World Report* (Nov. 13, 1961).

C.I.P.A.
Publications

The following publications are available from the University of Toronto Press:

The New Europe, ed. D. L. B. Hamlin. Based on the 31st Couchiching Conference, 1962. Pp. xii, 108, $2.00.
   Articles by: Raymond Aron, John Holmes, William Clark, William Diebold Jr., Shaun Herron, C. R. Ford, Eric Pettersson, A. W. Gillespie, Vladimir Velebit, Rudolf Meimberg, Charles Caccia, Peter Munk, Henry Mhun, Peyton Lyon, Jan Tupker, Harry Wolfson.

The Press and the Public, ed. D.L.B. Hamlin. Based on the 8th Winter Conference, 1962. Pp. x, 38, $1.50.
   Articles by: Louis M. Lyons, Stuart Keate, Robert Fulford.

Diplomacy in Evolution, ed. D. L. B. Hamlin. Based on the 30th Couchiching Conference, 1961. Pp. viii, 128, $2.00.
   Articles by: Ritchie Calder, Gordon Coburn, André Philip, H. R. Vohra, Harry Wolfson, John Holmes, Henry Kissinger, Geoffrey Bourne, G. R. Davy, Gordon Hawkins, C. B. Marshall, John Polanyi, James Eayrs, Duff Roblin.

The Price of Being Canadian, ed. D. L. B. Hamlin. Based on the 7th Winter Conference, 1961. Pp. x, 54, $1.50.
   Articles by: Douglas V. LePan, Hugh MacLennan, Frank Underhill, André Raynauld.

The following publications are available from the Canadian Institute on Public Affairs, 244 St. George St., Toronto, Ont.:

Is Business Reshaping Society?, ed. D. L. B. Hamlin. Based on the 6th Winter Conference, 1960. Pp. viii, 56, $1.00.
   Articles by: Earle MacPhee, W. H. Evans, Maurice Lamontagne, Pierre Berton, Ian McRae, W. P. Scott, W. E. Williams, A. W. Gillespie, J. R. M. Wilson, Herbert Lank, Stanley Knowles, B. S. Keirstead, Adolf Berle Jr., T. W. Kent, Monteath Douglas.

Crisis: '58, ed. Catherine D. McLean. Based on the 27th Couchiching Conference, 1958. Pp. iv, 100, $1.00.
   Articles by: Lester Pearson, Fritz Erler, Robert Bowie, Thomas A. Mann, Ellis A. Johnson, Robert McKenzie, Chan Htoon, Eugene Forsey, A. D. Misener, Gerald Graham.